CAROL KENT

# Detours, Tow Trucks, and Angels in Disguise

## Finding Humor and Hope in Unexpected Places

BRINGING TRUTH TO LIFE
NavPress Publishing Group
P.O. Box 35001, Colorado Springs, Colorado 80935

The Navigators is an international Christian organization. Our mission is to reach, disciple, and equip people to know Christ and to make Him known through successive generations. We envision multitudes of diverse people in the United States and every other nation who have a passionate love for Christ, live a lifestyle of sharing Christ's love, and multiply spiritual laborers among those without Christ.

NavPress is the publishing ministry of The Navigators. NavPress publications help believers learn biblical truth and apply what they learn to their lives and ministries. Our mission is to stimulate spiritual formation among our readers.


Library of Congress Catalog Card Number: 96-12541
ISBN 08910-99743

Cover illustration: Jared Lee

The following chapters were originally published in *Speak Up with Confidence* and are used with permission of the publisher (Thomas Nelson).

Big Lips
I Love Chocolate!
The Happy Mohawk Canoe Trip
High Heels and Tennis Shoes
Jonathan's Story

"Tiny Tim" is a copyrighted unpublished story by Sharon Dunsmore, as told to Carol Kent. All reprint permissions for this story must be secured from Sharon Dunsmore. Used by permission.

Most of the ancedotal illustrations in this book are true to life and are included with the permission of the persons involved. In some cases, names and identifying details have been changed to protect the privacy of the people involved, and any resemblance to people living or dead is coincidental.



Kent, Carol, 1947–
Detours, tow trucks, and angels in disguise : finding humor and hope in unexpected places / Carol Kent.
p. cm.
ISBN 0-89109-974-3 (pbk.)
1. Meditations. 2. Christian life—Anecdotes. 3. Christian life—Humor. 4. Kent, Carol, 1947– . I. Title.
BV4832.2.K44 1996 96-12541
242—dc20 CIP

Printed in the United States of America

1 2 3 4 5 6 7 8 9 10 11 12 13 14 15 / 99 98 97 96

# Contents

This book is lovingly dedicated to my sister
Jennie Afman Dimkoff

---

*The day you were born I became a sister.*
*We were buddies from the start.*
*Thank you for loving me so unselfishly.*
*My memory bank is filled with Kodak moments*
*of our growing up years together.*
*We truly believed God could take ordinary girls like us*
*and do His extraordinary work*
*if we wholeheartedly gave Him our potential.*
*We're grown women now, and when I look at you,*
*I marvel at His handiwork.*
*Thank you for believing in my wildest dreams*
*and for celebrating with me when God does the impossible*
*again . . . and again . . . and again.*
*I love you.*

# Acknowledgments

While attending an insurance convention with my husband, I listened as the president of the company gave his farewell address before making his retirement official. He said, "Many people have asked me to define the secret of my success. It's very simple. *I have made a lifetime habit of surrounding myself with people who are more successful than I am.*"

Although those words have a "secular ring," I have discovered some potent analogies in my spiritual life. I'd like to salute the people who use their gifts to free me to do what God has called me to do.

I am in the debt of the following exceptional people:

**The NavPress Publishing Team**

Thank you for believing in my potential and taking a risk on me a few years ago. I value your professional input, but beyond that, I thank God for your deep concern for the spiritual impact of my projects.

Liz Heaney, you are an editorial genius. Confrontive. Tough. Honest. Affirming. Encouraging. This manuscript has your remarkable influence on every page.

**The Individuals Who Shared Their Stories**

A project like this requires input from many people who are willing to be vulnerable, candid, and accessible. Without you, this book could not have been written. "Hats off" to: family members, Clyde and Pauline Afman, Jennie Afman Dimkoff, Bonnie Emmorey, Ben Afman, and Joy Carlson. And friends: Harley and Johnnie Sowell, Carole Clark, Vern and Betty Ens, Dr. Don Denmark, Ace and Sheri Spencer, Mary G. Block, Daisy Cross, Donna Jon Goddard, Bill and Pam Mutz, Dr. and Mrs. David Miller, Linda Miller, Lee and Sue Black, and Sharon Dunsmore. Thank you for offering humor and hope to people who need to see God's hand at work in everyday experiences. Additional thanks goes to Nan Walker and countless others who prayed during the writing of this manuscript.

**My Assistant**

Laurie Dennis, you freed me from an administrative nightmare so I could complete this project. Thank you for gracing my office with your extraordinary ability to "get things done!"

**My Family**

Gene Kent, you could write the book on "how to be a husband." You are strong in areas where I am weak. You lift my spirits when I'm discouraged. You are my best friend.

J.P. (Jason Paul), how could any parent be more proud of a son? This book is liberally sprinkled with life lessons you have taught me. I know God has big plans for your future!

❧

Diligent effort has been made to find the source of all material used in this book. However, I have gathered many unidentified clippings that have been faxed or mailed to me from all over the world. If you know the correct source for items now labeled "Source unknown," please contact me (address given on page 204) so that proper credit can be given in future printings.

# Why I Wrote This Book and What You'll Get Out of It

Okay, I admit it! I thought if I called this section the introduction, you might skip it—and I really want you to know why I wrote this book, so please read this first.

An old Arab proverb says, "The best speaker is he who turns ears into eyes."[1] It's true. Illustrations make truth memorable. Through my many years of teaching and speaking, I have learned that people often remember my main point because a key story captivated their attention and allowed them to personalize that point. Stories are word pictures that help us visualize an event or situation. They allow us to feel emotions we might never experience if we only heard the facts—and then they invite us to apply what we have learned.

Walt Disney was a master at captivating our imagination. A dreamer and a risk-taker, he created unforgettable stories. I quoted the following story about him in my book *Speak Up with Confidence*, and I repeat it here because it has influenced the writing of this book.

> Years ago Walt Disney discovered an important ingredient in successful feature-length animated cartoons. *Snow White* was a huge success, but other films that followed, although equally well constructed from a technical viewpoint, never did as well. Disney's team tried to analyze

> what made the difference. They made an incredible discovery! Every one of the truly successful productions, the films that people would pay to see again and again, had two ingredients—laughter and tears! Everything they did from that point on had to have both elements before it was released.[2]

God designed us to see, feel, hear, touch, cry, and hope. When we hear a story that allows us to "connect" on an emotional level, we internalize the meaning and personalize the message.

Most of my life I have learned the lesson God wanted to teach me only when I looked into the rear-view mirror of time. Through my unexpected detours on the journey of life, I've met people God used to teach me profound truth. Sometimes it's months or even years after experiencing a life event that I figure out the "why." It might be a conflict with my husband or son, or the loss of a loved one, or a major accident, or holding the hand of a friend in a hospital bed, or a vacation that became a fiasco, or going through an embarrassing situation that brought total humiliation. Later, as I view the situation in the light of God's Word and ask Him to reveal what He wants to teach me through the event, situation, or person—*only then do I discover the truth He wanted me to learn.*

The stories in this book have all been written as seen through time's rear-view mirror. I've included them to give you hope. Some of my "detours" will make you laugh and others may cause you to wipe a tear. They are illustrations you can retell a friend who needs a lifeline and a reminder that God is at work on the "daily days."

Since I'm busy and you're busy, I've written short chapters so you can read them in a few minutes or over a period of days or weeks or months. You won't have to reserve time to read a full-length chapter in one sitting in order to get the benefit.

Even though your stories are not my stories, I hope you will begin to evaluate your own life in the light of God's Word and His divine purpose. The biblical quotation at the end of each story points to an eternal perspective that offers us hope and joy amid the difficulties and disappointments of life in this fallen world.

It's my prayer that by the time you finish reading this book, you will be tuning in to your own stories and asking God to show you the life lessons He wants you to discover as you take your own detours along the way.

If you have children at home, I hope you will take time at dinner to talk with them about the day's events and help them discover God's meaning in the events in their lives. Have a brainstorming session after the evening meal and try to find a Bible verse that demonstrates God's application for the situations they encounter. Remember Moses' advice to the children of Israel:

> Only be careful, and watch yourselves closely so that you do not forget the things your eyes have seen or let them slip from your heart as long as you live. Teach them to your children and to their children after them. (Deuteronomy 4:9)

If you find that this book lifts your heart, pass it on to a friend. I encourage you to cultivate your own heart-lifters by developing the daily habit of finding God in the experiences you encounter during an ordinary day. If you open your eyes and see the potential in today's interruption, you just might meet an angel in disguise. Watch out! Your life may never be the same again!

PART ONE

# When God Surprises

ONE

# The Wrecker Driver

I PACKED MY BAGS and jumped into the car for the three-hour trip to a Christian Women's Club luncheon. After I spoke, several women made the decision to begin a faith-walk with Jesus Christ as their personal Savior. With spirits soaring, I thought, *Life doesn't get much better than this!*

Back in the car, I drove another hour to Lansing, Michigan, where I planned to spend the night with the woman who had been my best friend throughout high school. We anticipated an evening of food, fun, and catching up on our lives before I left for a speaking engagement in Ohio the next morning.

Because I usually bypassed downtown Lansing on trips across the state, I was unfamiliar with the traffic patterns within the city. My stress mounted as I traversed unknown streets, realizing that rush hour had begun. I stopped at a red light and was about to hit the accelerator when the light turned green, and my engine died.

Within seconds, impatient people were honking their horns—the light had turned and they wanted to move *now!* I desperately attempted to start the car. Nothing happened. Angry drivers began making their way around my vehicle, mouthing words at me through the windows—and I could tell they were *not* quoting Bible verses! (How I wished I had registered for the class in auto mechanics instead of taking home economics.)

I pleaded: "Lord, You are the God of miracles. You fed all of those people with that little boy's lunch. Compared to the big stuff You've done, it would be a small thing for You to zap this engine and get my car moving again. Would You please get this car started?" I turned the key in the ignition. Nothing happened.

I began to realize this situation called for a different type of prayer. Placing my hands on the steering wheel with authority, I prayed loudly, "God, what are *You* going to do with *Your* car? You and I have to be in Ohio tomorrow! How will *we* get there?" I thought if I switched ownership to Him, He would feel more responsibility to get involved in helping to solve my problem. Again, I turned the key in the ignition, and the car started—and kept running just long enough to get me out of the intersection and into a side street where there was less traffic. At that point no amount of begging or pleading with God seemed to make any difference to my stalled engine.

I went to the door of a nearby home and asked if I could use the telephone. The woman spoke only Spanish. I've had three years of French and two years of Latin, but I don't know Spanish. With the help of sign language, she finally understood that I needed a phone, and she led me to her kitchen where I called a wrecker service. After such a great beginning, this was turning out to be a very bad day!

When the wrecker pulled up, I was surprised to see a *female* driver. This woman knew her business. She hoisted my car into place, and I jumped into the cab as she began driving toward the service garage. As we rode down the highway, I haltingly questioned, "I hope you don't mind if I ask. You're very skilled at what you do. How did you get into this line of work?"

Peering in my direction, she smiled. "To tell you the truth, I have a bachelor of arts degree in Russian literature, and I'm working on a master's degree in theology right now." The shocked look on my face did not startle her. She continued, "At this time last year I was working overseas in a Communist country in underground evangelism."

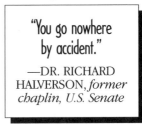

> "You go nowhere by accident."
>
> —DR. RICHARD HALVERSON, *former chaplin, U.S. Senate*

With astonishment, I said, "You mean, *you're a Christian?*"

"Yeah! You too?"

I exclaimed, "Yeah! Me too!"

As we talked, she told me it had been the most difficult year of her life. She was headed for the mission field, and her heart longed to be there. But she had university debts and needed to pay her bills before she went into full-time ministry. Becoming a wrecker driver was the fastest way she could make the necessary funds to take care of her obligations. But it was hard. She bore the brunt of malicious comments and snide remarks from people who thought a female wrecker driver was a joke.

We pulled into the driveway of the service garage, and I found myself giving comfort and encouragement to my wrecker driver. Her passion for God was obvious, but she was discouraged. We prayed out loud together in the cab of that truck, and I gave her a hug before we said goodbye.

As I stepped out of the service garage, I realized the home of my high school friend was located right across the street. I didn't even need to call a cab. I walked across the street, knocked on the door of my very surprised friend, and related the story of this unusual day. It seemed even more of a miracle that by calling the first service garage I found in the yellow pages, I happened to select one that was right across the street from my destination.

The next morning I crossed the street and walked into the garage and asked the service manager if they had discovered what was wrong with my car. He scratched his head as he responded, "Lady, we've taken your automobile through every kind of test we have, and there's nothing wrong with it. It runs just fine, and we have no idea why you had a problem with it yesterday."

As I drove to the Ohio conference, God spoke to my heart: "Carol, you are My ambassador. Yesterday, I had a lonely, discouraged wrecker driver in Lansing, Michigan, who desperately needed to be reminded that I care about her and I have a plan for her life beyond her present difficult circumstances. You had a little extra time, and I picked you to be the one to pray with her and give her a message of encouragement."

I thought back to the day before. I had been impatient. Angry. Upset with God. My carefully made plans were interrupted. My precious schedule was being altered by a situation that seemed beyond my control. I was mad at God for allowing my car to have problems when I was trying to do His work faithfully.

At that moment, I realized that almost every day I have *interruptions* that are actually *God-appointments* in disguise. I wondered how many opportunities I had missed in the past because I saw only the interruption.

*I am the LORD your God,*
*who teaches you what is best for you,*
*who directs you in the way you should go.*
*If only you had paid attention to my commands,*
*your peace would have been like a river,*
*your righteousness like the waves of the sea.*

Isaiah 48:17-18

TWO

# A Surprise Ending

WHEN I WAS A BABY, my father sensed God's call on his life for the ministry. He went to Bible school for a while and then, as economic pressures increased, he dropped out, intending to go back.

Years passed. Mom and Dad had four more children, and Dad got a job as an agent for the New York Life Insurance Company, where he made a good living.

The year I began junior high, we got a new minister at our church. He preached a series of sermons on Jonah—the biblical leader who tried to run away from God's instructions. My father identified with this disobedient prophet and he was *miserable!* After church one Sunday my father was weeping—and that almost *never* happened. Mother and Dad went behind closed doors and were having an intense conversation. My curiosity got the best of me. Putting my ear to the door, I listened to the voices inside the next room.

Through tears, my father said, "Pauline, I'm either going to comply with God's will and go into the ministry, or I'm going to have to get out of church work completely. I can't go on like this!" In the next moment, my mother burst into tears. (I later found out they were *joyful* tears.) Then reality hit me. *I was going to become a preacher's kid!* I had heard horror stories of life inside the glass fishbowl of the pastor's home. The news seemed like a death sentence.

During the next few months I observed my parents carefully. Dad enrolled in Bible school. Then he made an appointment with his boss, a man who did not know the Lord. After my father greeted his employer warmly, he sat across the desk from him and stated the reason for the appointment. "I know agents in the company are full-time employees, but God has called me to preach, and I have enrolled in Bible school. If there is any possibility of working here part time so I can feed my family while I'm preparing for the ministry, I would be very grateful."

My father's employer leaned back in his chair and thoughtfully scratched his head. He spoke slowly and carefully. "Well, Clyde, as far as I'm concerned, you can go to school full time and keep your regular paycheck as long as your sales keep up."

During the entire time my father finished his education and prepared for the ministry, his sales in that business were higher than they had ever been before. I watched God meet all of the *needs* of our growing family—not all of the *wants*—and we never lacked for food or basic necessities.

When I was fourteen years old and about to enter high school, Dad accepted the invitation to pastor his first church. There were forty-two people in that first little congregation—seven of them from our family.

I had four years of piano lessons under my belt, so I became the church pianist. There were often major hesitations between my chords, but I practiced long and hard and made some headway, finally conquering the song "Dwelling in Beulah Land." It was written in the key of B-flat, and still sounded like music even when I pounded the same chords repeatedly. We sang that song almost every week while I slowly added to my limited repertoire. No one called my contribution *music*, but it *was* "a joyful noise."

Mother and Dad made home visits a priority, and many men and women came to Christ. Within a year that little congregation had more than doubled. One of my father's favorite ministry activities was a concept he borrowed from his insurance career. He enjoyed doing "cold canvass calling." That meant he showed up on people's doorsteps without making an appointment first. He liked the casual atmosphere this produced and found it made sharing the gospel in a natural setting a little bit easier.

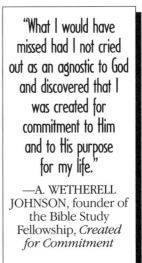

> "What I would have missed had I not cried out as an agnostic to God and discovered that I was created for commitment to Him and to His purpose for my life."
>
> —A. WETHERELL JOHNSON, founder of the Bible Study Fellowship, *Created for Commitment*

One day Dad was visiting parishioners in the local hospital. He stopped in a room unexpectedly and met Francis Kent. Dad sensed that Francis was hungry for spiritual meaning in his life and decided to meet with him at a later date. A few weeks passed and Francis was released from the hospital.

On New Year's Day my father thought about this man again and asked if I would baby-sit while he and Mother visited Francis and his family. Baby-sitting was *not* my favorite activity. Grudgingly, I agreed to baby-sit my four younger sisters and my brother while Mom and Dad visited with the Kents.

After they arrived, Mom and Dad sat around a little kitchen table and shared the plan of salvation with Francis and his wife. Just as they were about to invite Christ into their lives, their seventeen-year-old son stuck his head around the corner. He hesitantly said, "I'm sorry for interrupting, but I've been listening in on this conversation, and I wonder if I could become a Christian, too." That night young Gene Kent joined his parents in prayer and made the decision to make Christ the center of his life.

When Mom and Dad got home and told me that Gene Kent had just become a Christian, I GOT EXCITED! For several years my father had been announcing, "There will be absolutely no dating of nonChristians for my five daughters!" That was a problem. We lived in a very small town, and we were in a very small church. At that point there were eight girls in the church youth group—and only two guys. One of them was so unattractive you prayed he wouldn't ask you to go out on a date. And the other one was so "drop-dead gorgeous" you could get killed in the stampede of women running after his admiring glance. I couldn't believe there was now a third possibility in the form of handsome, dynamic, intelligent Gene Kent!

That day, while I was at home doing the mundane, ordinary, not-very-much-loved job of baby-sitting and nothing exceptional seemed to be happening in my life, my mother and father were out winning my future husband to Jesus Christ! And from that day to this I've discovered some of God's best surprises happen on my *daily* days.

***So let's not allow ourselves***
***to get fatigued doing good.***
***At the right time we will harvest a good crop***
***if we don't give up, or quit.***
***Right now, therefore, every time we get the chance,***
***let us work for the benefit of all,***
***starting with the people closest to us.***

Galatians 6:9-10, MSG

THREE

# The Atheist's Daughter

GENE AND I HAD just been seated at our table in the elegant hotel ballroom. We were attending a formal awards dinner for the sales force of the insurance company my husband works for.

Introductions were made and we found ourselves sitting next to a delightful couple from the great Northwest—Seattle, Washington. Bob and Susan were energetic, highly motivated, and entertaining. When they found out we were Christians too, they openly told us how they came to know Christ.

Susan grew up in the home of an atheist. From the time she was a little girl, her father said, "Susan, watch out for those overly aggressive Christians. They carry big Bibles and preach at you all the time."

Susan didn't think much about God or spiritual issues during her growing-up years. She left for college and soon met Bob. Bob was from a nonreligious home, too. They had a lot in common and before long they fell in love and, later, married. They were extremely happy.

One day Susan was in line at the grocery store, waiting to check out. The two women in front of her were obviously friends. As they stood waiting for their change, Susan heard one say to the other, "You know, you really shouldn't reject the Bible if you haven't even read it."

Susan never met either of the women, but that thought haunted her: *You really shouldn't reject the Bible if you haven't even read it.* She was an educated woman and an avid reader. She had read the classics and the best sellers, but she had never even picked up a Bible.

She couldn't stop thinking about what she heard, and on the way home she stopped by the public library and checked out a copy of the Holy Bible. When evening came, she and Bob got ready for bed and Susan began reading the Bible out loud to Bob, beginning in Genesis. She read until he fell asleep, and then she read further, until she got sleepy.

> "We are free to either love God or not. He invites us to love Him. He urges us to love Him. He came that we might love Him. But, in the end, the choice is yours and mine."
>
> —MAX LUCADO, *And the Angels Were Silent*

Every night Susan read aloud to Bob, beginning where she'd left off the night before. She read until he fell asleep, then she read silently until her eyelids got heavy. (They made it through Genesis, Exodus, Leviticus, Numbers, and Deuteronomy. When I read through the Bible, I usually die out mentally somewhere in the middle of Leviticus, and I've been a Christian for many years! *Their persistence was remarkable!*)

They had almost finished the Old Testament when, one day, Susan was walking along the sidewalk and saw a gospel tract entitled "Four Things God Wants You to Know" on the ground. Susan picked it up and, as she read, her eyes fell on these words: "(1) God loves you. (2) Sin separates you from God. (3) Jesus, God's Son, through His death on the cross, paid the price for your sin, and He rose again. (4) To receive His gift of salvation, you need to confess your sin and invite Him to be your Savior."

There was a prayer printed at the bottom of the page. Susan's heart was so prepared for this moment by the reading of God's Word and by the Spirit of God that she bowed her head and invited Christ into her life right there and then.

A couple of weeks later, she and Bob were invited to a home for dinner with some new friends. When they arrived, they discovered several other couples were guests as well. They enjoyed a gourmet meal and a very entertaining evening. As they left the house, Bob paused on the sidewalk between the house and the car. Turning to Susan, he said, "Honey, I think those people have something that we need, but I can't figure out what it is."

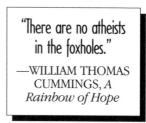

> "There are no atheists in the foxholes."
>
> —WILLIAM THOMAS CUMMINGS, *A Rainbow of Hope*

Susan spoke softly. "Bob," she whispered, "I think I found it." As they got into their car, Susan opened her purse and pulled out the tattered gospel tract. "I found this piece of paper on the sidewalk a couple of weeks ago and I did what it said. Let me tell you about it."

She began reading it aloud. "God loves you. Sin separates you from God. Jesus, God's Son, died on the cross and paid the price for our sin and He rose again. To receive His gift of salvation, you need to confess your sin, and invite Him to be your Savior."

The reading of the Word of God and the Spirit of God working in his heart had prepared Bob's heart for the truth of the gospel. He bowed his head in that car and invited Jesus Christ to be his Savior.

Bob and Susan discovered that God is in the business of changing lives. They soon found a church that taught the Bible, and today they are active members, rearing their three children to love and serve the Lord.

By the time they returned the Holy Bible to the public library, they had a ten-dollar overdue fine on it!

*God means what he says.*
*What he says goes.*
*His powerful Word is sharp*
*as a surgeon's scalpel,*
*cutting through everything,*
*whether doubt or defense,*
*laying us open to listen and obey.*
*Nothing and no one is impervious to God's Word.*
*We can't get away from it—no matter what.*

Hebrews 4:12, MSG

FOUR

# No Solution in Sight

MANY TIMES EVENTS and circumstances have seemed out of my control. *Something* or *somebody* has upset my carefully made plans, and I feel powerless and upset. In my heart I yell, "Lord, where are You? I do not see Your purpose in this situation. I'm in a problem and I do not see a solution!"

One of these times occurred on July 26, my wedding day. Four years of dating and months of planning had led up to this important day. Gene and I had spent hours memorizing special vows we were going to share with each other as we exchanged rings. Our vows would be the most sacred part of the ceremony, a testimony to all who attended the event.

It was a *family* affair! I'm the oldest of six children. Three of my sisters were bridesmaids; my youngest sister was the flower girl, and my only brother, dressed in a miniature tuxedo, proudly stood as the ring bearer. My father is a preacher and we wanted him to marry us, so we arranged for a friend of the family to lead the service until Dad "gave me away."

Everything was progressing as planned. The processional began and my attendants made their way down the aisle. Then I heard the music I'd been waiting for, the distinctive, stately chords of "The Wedding March." This was *my* moment. People were standing and looking toward me at the back of the church. I took the arm of my tall, handsome father and began the carefully practiced "hesitation step" down the immaculate, white runway. I fixed my eyes on my gorgeous groom, the "main man" waiting for me at the end of this walk.

How could any event be more perfect? The music was inspiring. Significant people from our past had traveled vast distances to witness this merger of two people who had dedicated their lives to God and to each other. We had kept our relationship pure and desired to have this ceremony be a testimony of God's goodness and love.

But during the prayer before Dad was to "give me away," I panicked as I realized something. "Dad, Dad," I whispered, tugging on his arm, "I've forgotten the ring!"

In the excitement of getting pictures taken with my attendants and greeting family members and friends who stopped by to say hello, I had totally forgotten the ring! I had left it in the dressing room. I had *nothing* to give during the special vows we had memorized for the ring exchange. I was convinced I had ruined the entire ceremony!

Without hesitation, my father began removing his own wedding ring. (I found out later it was the first time in twenty-three years he had taken the ring off.) Dad tenderly took my hand, opened my nervous fingers, and placed *his* wedding ring in the palm of my hand. Then he carefully wrapped my fingers around the ring, and with a loving squeeze, I knew my father was telling me, *"Carol, everything is going to be okay!"*

That day my earthly father reminded me that I have a loving heavenly Father who has control of all the details of my life.

*God met me more than halfway,*
*he freed me from my anxious fears.*

*Look at him; give him your warmest smile.*
*Never hide your feelings from him.*

*When I was desperate, I called out,*
*and God got me out of a tight spot.*

*God's angel sets up a circle*
*of protection around us while we pray.*

*Open your mouth and taste, open your eyes*
*and see—how good God is.*
*Blessed are you who run to him.*

Psalm 34:4-8, MSG

*My sister Joy and her four-year-old son, K.C., were eating a lunch of butter sandwiches when Joy decided to turn this mealtime into a teachable moment. She wanted to see what K.C.'s keen little mind could conjure up in response to a series of theological questions about authority and submission.*

*In between bites she asked him simply, "Son, who is the boss of you?"*

*His voice sounded confident. "You, Mommy."*

*So far, so good. Her next question built on the first. "And who is the boss of Mommy?"*

*This question was not answered as swiftly as the first, but he finally managed to come up with a satisfactory answer. "Daddy," he replied, somewhat hesitantly.*

*"And who," she questioned, "is the boss of Daddy?"*

*She was searching for a very simple answer, indicating K.C. understood that God is our final authority. She wasn't expecting him to go up the authority ladder with responses like "church leadership" or "human government."*

*K.C. was struggling hard to come up with the correct answer. There was a definite question mark at the end of his answer. He replied, "Grandma and Grandpa?"*

*That answer was good enough to induce a chuckle from Joy.*

*However, a few hints later my nephew was able to come up with the response his mother was looking for—"God."*

*Joy couldn't stop there. She had one last question that would really tell her how her son was thinking. "Son, who will be the boss of you when you're a grownup?"*

*This question produced the greatest anxiety of all. K.C. took his time to ponder the question. Then, with great apprehension, he looked up with a furrowed brow and responded, "My wife?"*

PART TWO

# When All You Can Do Is Laugh

FIVE

# Big Lips

IT HAPPENED IN fourth grade. I was sitting in my seat looking at my teacher, priding myself—as always—on being a good student. John, in the seat behind me, tapped me on the shoulder. I'd been noticing him for quite some time, hoping he would notice me too. I turned around in my seat, put on my best smile, and said softly, "Yes?"

> "A healthy self-image is seeing yourself as God sees you—no more and no less."
>
> —JOSH MCDOWELL, *Building Your Self-Image*

He didn't say anything; he just stared at something on my face. Then he elbowed the fellow next to him and whispered, "See?"

This fellow also began to stare at something on my face and replied, "Yeah, I see."

The initiator of the conversation then proceeded to say, "She *does* have big lips, doesn't she?"

I was devastated. I turned around in my seat, pretending it didn't matter, all the while breaking out in a nervous red rash. Finally, the bell rang, and I ran outside, boarded the bus, and found a quiet seat in the back.

When the bus stopped in front of my house, I jumped off and ran in the front door and up the stairs to my second-story bedroom; I threw myself across the bed and sobbed. I knew I was the homeliest girl in the entire world. I was certain I'd never be asked out on a date. I knew I would never be married. And I also doubted that I would ever be gainfully employed. Who would hire a girl with lips like *these* to work in a business establishment?

I decided that in order to get what I wanted from life, I'd have to become one of the thin-lipped people. Whenever I had leisure time, I would stand in front of my mirror and painstakingly roll my lips inward until they were thin and beautiful. But I discovered a brand-new problem: It is almost impossible to speak with "thin" lips (at least with big lips rolled in to look thinner)! I began practicing at home with my "new" mouth, perfecting my speech before my public debut.

One day my father looked at me and said, "Carol, *what on earth are you doing to your mouth?*"

To this day, there are moments when I involuntarily begin to pull in my lips—because of one unkind comment of a boy in my fourth-grade classroom.

***A word out of your mouth***
***may seem of no account,***
***but it can accomplish nearly anything—***
***or destroy it!***

***It only takes a spark,***
***remember, to set off a forest fire.***
***A careless or wrongly placed word***
***out of your mouth can do that.***
***By our speech we can ruin the world,***
***turn harmony to chaos,***
***throw mud on a reputation,***
***send the whole world up in smoke***
***and go up in smoke with it.***

James 3:5-6, MSG

SIX

# The Dead Cat

I NEVER KNEW if Uncle Jake was in mid-life crisis or if he acted a little crazy just because he was born that way. He was balding and his hair formed a semicircle that surrounded his head like a misplaced halo. He kept a few hairs long so they could be combed directly across his bald spot. (I recently read that you know a man is in mid-life crisis when he begins wearing his sideburns on top of his head.)

Uncle Jake was one of my favorite relatives. He was one of eleven children, all of whom had children of their own. At last count, I had almost fifty first cousins on that side of the family alone. He attracted children like nobody else, and my cousins and I especially adored his wildly funny stories about his wife, our beloved Aunt Deal. She was the one relative who always remembered to put money in our birthday cards.

We never knew if Uncle Jake's stories were fact or fiction, and we didn't care. Uncle Jake told stories with dynamic body language and a full range of inflection. During those splendid reunions, we begged him to repeat our favorite scenario. I remember sitting at his feet, waiting for little laugh lines to form around his twinkling eyes as he mesmerized us with that particular wild tale. It goes like this.

One day when Aunt Deal left the house for work, she had a little extra time and decided to run a quick errand at the local shopping mall. As she carefully backed the car out of the driveway, she felt an unnerving *thump, thump* as her tires ran over something.

She stopped the vehicle abruptly and jumped out of the front seat to discover she had just run over the family cat. The limp, lifeless cat had met with an untimely death—and Aunt Deal was distraught. Some animals are a friendly nuisance—but this animal was like a member of the family!

She knew her children would get home after school, just before she returned from work, and they would be *devastated* if they found their pet in this terminated condition. Aunt Deal *couldn't* throw the cat in the garbage can. Not knowing what to do and wanting to show respect for such a valued pet, she decided to delay the decision until she could talk to Uncle Jake about how to tell the children and how to give the cat a proper burial. She grabbed a shopping bag out of the kitchen, placed the dead cat in the bag, and put the bag on the back seat. By the time she reached the shopping mall, the temperature had escalated. The parking lot was nearly full; she found a spot for her car near the end of one of the long lines of automobiles.

Knowing that the rising temperature would cause the cat to stink, she decided to take the bag out of the car and place it on the hood where it would be in the open air while she went into the store to pick up a few items.

Minutes later when she emerged from the store, she saw an obese woman standing next to the car. The woman nervously looked to her right and then to her left, and promptly grabbed that shopping bag and began walking briskly in the direction of the stores.

Aunt Deal thought, *I can't miss this!* and followed her.

The woman passed three storefronts before she decided to check out her "find." As she reached down into the bottom of the bag, the expression on her face changed from glee to horror. When she realized the fur was not a stole but a dead cat, the woman keeled over. Someone in the crowd yelled, "This woman's fainted! Call for an ambulance!"

> "A well-developed sense of humor is the pole that adds balance to your steps as you walk the tightrope of life."
>
> —WILLIAM A. WARD, *Quotable Quotations*

Within a short time, the rescue team arrived. The emergency workers laid the still-unconscious woman out on the stretcher. After they worked over her feverishly, they rolled the stretcher into the back of the ambulance. At that moment, someone in the crowd yelled, "That bag is hers!" One of the rescue workers picked up the shopping bag and placed it on the woman's belly. And with sirens blaring, they drove off.

Uncle Jake never did tell us what the woman did when she woke up and saw the bag, but we were all convinced that if she lived, *she never stole again!* Aunt Deal denied the incident ever happened. Uncle Jake, with that knowing, mischievous twinkle in his eye, insisted it did.

I still believe him.

***A cheerful heart brings a smile to your face;***
***a sad heart makes it hard to get through***
***the day.***

Proverbs 15:13, MSG

SEVEN

# Living by the Book

I RECEIVED MY UNDERGRADUATE degree from one of the strictest universities in the country. We could not hold hands with the opposite sex on campus. Our hemlines had to be a certain length, and women could wear slacks only when going to the tennis courts and returning to the dormitory—nowhere else! We sometimes joked that one of us might be the first student shipped home because the dean of women found a hole in the *knee* of our bathing suit.

I didn't mind the rules too much, but my best friend, Terry, struggled with them. Only two weeks after we arrived she was caught holding hands with her boyfriend. She was sent a slip of paper indicating she had an appointment with the dean of women. Only a very serious offense would necessitate a meeting with the dean. I was nervous for my friend.

Terry entered the dean's office and was asked to sit down across from her at the desk. It was a long, impressive desk, with the wooden finish polished so perfectly you could see your reflection. The dean looked at Terry with penetrating steely gray eyes and spoke in a slow, Southern drawl: "My dear girl, what are you *saving* for marriage?"

Terry was so surprised by the question she felt like

responding enthusiastically, "Why, I'm saving *the other hand*, ma'am."

Somehow, she squelched her immediate thought, and the dean of women proceeded with her comments. "Well, dear, maybe that's why I've never been married, but my lips have *never* been defiled!"

Terry hadn't been caught kissing—just holding hands—but when she got back to the dorm and shared her wild tale, we all determined to avoid any "touching" encounters on the campus. They would definitely get us into too much trouble.

There were other rules. Chapel services were held five days a week and attendance was mandatory. One day our guest speaker was Dr. Charles Woodbridge. He had white hair and stately posture, and he seemed wise. He spoke with authority and held the Bible in his hands as if it were his most precious possession. I liked this man. He was passionate about God and his presentation left me challenged and convicted. I was hungry for the intimacy this man had with God.

Halfway through his message he must have noticed that the audience was preoccupied. There were about four thousand students in the auditorium that day. He spoke with great volume and intense fervor: "YOUNG PEOPLE, LOOK UP FROM YOUR BIBLES—PLEASE!"

At that moment four thousand heads looked up in unison, and Dr. Woodbridge continued. Each word was separated with a brief pause for emphasis. "YOUNG PEOPLE . . . IF YOU WANT TO *KNOW* THE WORD OF GOD, PICK ONE BOOK OF THE BIBLE—ANY BOOK—AND READ IT EVERY DAY FOR A MONTH. YOUR LIFE WILL *NEVER* BE THE SAME AGAIN!"

There was a boldness in this man that came right from the Holy Spirit and went straight to my heart. I had joked about all of the rules and regulations at the school, but I was challenged by these chapel services, and I decided to take the advice of Dr. Woodbridge.

I selected the book of Philippians for two reasons. I knew it was about *joy*—and as a university student living on limited funds, I needed more joy. The second reason was obvious. It's a *short* book. With only four chapters, I could read the whole book in about fifteen minutes. Even a very busy university student could find a quarter of an hour to read the Bible.

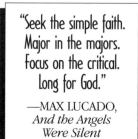

> "Seek the simple faith. Major in the majors. Focus on the critical. Long for God."
>
> —MAX LUCADO, *And the Angels Were Silent*

The first week, I read Philippians because I had made the commitment—and I always did what I said I would do. (I think it's a first-born, obsessive/compulsive thing!) By the second week I realized I was *enjoying the book*. I felt like Paul, the author of the book, was a personal friend. By the third week, I was memorizing long passages without even trying. And by the fourth week, Philippians had become my favorite book of the Bible. Falling in love with the Bible was a new experience for me.

Looking back on those four brief years of my life, I smile. Rules. Regulations. Regimented skirt lengths. Chaperoned dating. Room inspections. Mandatory chapel. None of it seemed pleasant or desirable, but it *did* challenge me to form opinions about what's right and wrong, good and bad, essential and nonessential. Did I enjoy the rules? No. Did they hurt me? Not really. Did I become cynical and warped because I had to "toe the line"? I don't think so.

And by the way, I've been married for a *long* time, and I *still* get a big thrill out of holding hands!

***Meanwhile, live in such a way that you are a credit to the Message of Christ.***

Philippians 1:27, MSG

EIGHT

# Husband for Sale

IT HAPPENED AGAIN. Gene and I were in the car running errands, and I felt he was too close to the car in front of us. As the other automobile slowed down unexpectedly, I shrieked, "WATCH OUT!" Gene slammed on the brakes and we were jolted forward.

As usual, he had plenty of room to stop, and we could have avoided this jerky reaction if I had kept my mouth shut. He was angry with me for being a back-seat driver—again. I told him I screamed because I honestly thought we were in danger and I believed my warning might save our lives. He was unconvinced. He pulled the car to the side of the road, looked in my direction, and said, "Do you want to drive?"

Now I was hurt. I wasn't trying to tell him how to drive. My scream had been involuntary. I did not plan to make him feel like an inadequate driver. Tears blocked my vision as I withdrew into my silent martyr role. (I feel so much more spiritual when I'm not speaking.) We drove home in the thick silence of anger, hurt, and misunderstanding.

As we mutely walked into the house, our conflict was still unresolved. I left Gene in the kitchen and walked into the next room. Opening my mail, I found this anonymous letter on my desk:

Dear Friend,

This letter was started by a woman like yourself in hopes of bringing relief to other tired and discontented women. Unlike most chain letters, this one does not cost anything.

Just bundle up your husband and send him to the woman whose name appears at the top of the list. Then add your name to the bottom of the list and send a copy of this letter to five of your friends who are equally tired and discontented. When your name comes to the top of the list, you will receive 3,325 men . . . and some of them are bound to be better than the one you gave up!

> "Laughing 100 times a day works the heart as much as exercising for ten minutes on a rowing machine."
>
> —A MEDICAL DOCTOR quoted by Barbara Johnson, *Stick a Geranium in Your Hat and Be Happy!*

DO NOT BREAK THIS CHAIN! One woman did, and she received her own jerk back!

At this writing, a friend of mine had already received 184 men. They buried her yesterday, but it took four undertakers thirty-six hours to get the smile off her face.

We're counting on you,
A Satisfied Woman[1]

By the time I reached the middle of the letter, I was grinning. As I finished it, I was doubled up in uproarious laughter. My confused husband walked into the room wondering what had transformed his wounded wife. Looking up, my eyes met his. "I'm sorry," I said softly. "I overreacted."

"Me, too," he responded, as he slipped an arm around my waist. His lips brushed the side of my face as he whispered in my ear, "Now, *what's so funny?*" His curiosity was killing him. And I couldn't keep a secret that was this hilarious.

"Listen to this," I said. I read the letter aloud, and both of us fell on the floor laughing until tears ran down our faces.

> ***Words kill, words give life;***
> ***they're either poison or fruit—you choose.***
>
> ***Find a good spouse, you find a good life—***
> ***and even more: the favor of GOD!***

Proverbs 18:21-22, MSG

NINE

# High Drama at the Bank

IT WAS A HOT, humid summer day. People were irritable and tired from the heat. My friend, Lee, was impatiently standing in line at the local bank.

A frazzled woman came up the walk. She was half carrying and half dragging her uncooperative son. He appeared to be about five years old, and he was *not* enjoying the opportunity of accompanying his mother on this trip to town. With the child in tow, the woman finally managed to make her way through the heavy doors at the entrance of the building.

> "Lord, when we are wrong, make us willing to change. And when we are right, make us easy to live with."
>
> —PETER MARSHALL, *A Rainbow of Hope*

In full view of all of the bank patrons, she set her shopping bags down and, with two hands, lifted her son in the air and carried him to one of the chairs in the waiting area. Exasperated, she plunked him down on the seat as she spoke in a voice that was audible to all: "I have *had it* with you today! I am *never* taking you shopping with me again! Don't you dare *move* until I come back to this spot! Do you understand me?"

The boy was startled enough to take her seriously. He nodded through tears. All eyes in the bank were on the child as he whimpered, "But, Mom, *you broke my . . . !*"

The bank patrons looked aghast! Had this mean mother been so rough on her child that she slammed him into the chair hard enough to cause physical damage? What kind of a child abuser *was* she? Visual daggers were shot in her direction from all parts of the lobby.

At that moment, to the surprise of all judgmental onlookers, the rambunctious child dug his hands into his back pockets and pulled out two totally flattened Ping-Pong balls.

***"Don't pick on people, jump on their failures, criticize their faults—unless, of course, you want the same treatment. That critical spirit has a way of boomeranging. It's easy to see a smudge on your neighbor's face and be oblivious to the ugly sneer on your own."***

Matthew 7:1-3, MSG

TEN

# I Love Chocolate!

I LOVE CHOCOLATE. I've told my husband that when I die, I'd like to be dipped in chocolate and then shipped off for burial in Hershey, Pennsylvania. I live in a house with two other chocoholics, so I have to have special hiding places for it. I keep some in the refrigerator; there's almost always some in the freezer; I keep a little in the Halloween treat candy jar on the top shelf of the cupboard; and a tin labeled Borwick's Baking Powder usually contains semisweet chocolate chips.

I was home recently and had planned to spend the day working. After jumping out of bed, I donned a pair of old slacks and a faded, well-worn sweater. I hurriedly brushed my hair, and I didn't put on any makeup. (Even relatives might not have recognized me that day. My sister Paula has a makeup case with printing on the side that says, "My face is in this bag." I needed that bag.)

Sitting down at my desk, I opened the Bible to Matthew 5, the text for my next retreat message, and I began a careful reading of the Beatitudes. I came to verse 6 and read, "Blessed are those who *hunger*." What do you guess I thought about?

I went to the refrigerator—no chocolate! I tried the freezer—no chocolate. The Halloween treat candy jar, too, was empty. I instinctively went to the pantry and pulled out the Borwick's Baking Powder can, knowing I had purchased chocolate chips just the week before. I reached inside and pulled a note from the bottom of the can: "Sorry, honey, I beat you to it!"

I was disappointed, but thought quickly, *Obviously, the Lord doesn't want me to have any chocolate this morning*. I reluctantly went back to my desk to concentrate on message preparation. After fifteen minutes I thought, *Why, it's only three miles to the store. I could be there and back in no time at all and satisfy this ridiculous craving*.

After making the decision to go to the store, I caught a glimpse of myself in the mirror. I didn't want to be seen looking like I did that morning. It took me at least half an hour to apply some makeup and put on appropriate clothing, so when I got to the store, I decided to make the trip worth my while. I picked up the largest Hershey's with almonds I could find; then I grabbed a giant-size Cadbury Caramello. (For those of you not into this sort of thing, that's chocolate and caramel together in one mouthwatering bite!) On my way to the check-out, I picked up the biggest bag of M & M's on the shelf.

As I walked out of the store and across the parking lot to my car, I consumed one-third of the Hershey's with almonds; on the three-mile trip home, I finished it off. I picked up the Cadbury. Thinking quickly, I realized that the M & M's would taste terrific with a big pot of coffee. I envisioned a delightful study time, sipping coffee and eating M & M's, one by one, all day. As the coffee in my drip pot worked its way to the bottom, I continued devouring the Cadbury. When I heard the final gurgle, signaling that the coffee was ready, I was finishing off the last bite of the second sixteen-ounce candy bar. At that moment, I realized I was so sick I could hardly move.

I'm ashamed to admit it, but that day, on a day I had reserved for Bible study, prayer, and preparation for ministry, I wound up wasting hours of precious time over a ridiculous human craving.

*So if you're serious about living this new resurrection life with Christ,* act *like it. Pursue the things over which Christ presides. Don't shuffle along, eyes to the ground, absorbed with the things right in front of you. Look up, and be alert to what is going on around Christ. . . . And that means killing off everything connected with that way of death: . . . doing whatever you feel like whenever you feel like it, and grabbing whatever attracts your fancy. That's a life shaped by things and feelings instead of by God.*

Colossians 3:1-2,5, MSG

*One Sunday evening as we were getting ready for church, God used my son to mirror for me how I sometimes come to God. I had bathed and dressed J.P. in a crisp, clean shirt and matching slacks. I then secured his brand-new white tennis shoes with their distinctive Velcro fasteners. I noticed that three unruly hairs were still standing straight up along his cowlick, so I carefully sprayed them down until they submitted to my authority. The kid looked "picture perfect."*

*With about five minutes to go before I could declare myself ready for the trip to church, I gave J.P. permission to go outside—with these instructions: "You can walk around the back yard while Mama gets ready for church, but don't go near the creek!" (Actually it was a drainage ditch, but we called it a creek in hopes that the property value would be increased!)*

*I hurriedly ran a brush through my hair and touched up my makeup. Minutes later I headed for the door—but the sight before my eyes was unnerving. There he stood, displaying the marks of disobedience: he was covered with green slime, he was wet, his tennis shoes were muddy, he had a bloody scratch from a tree limb, and all three hairs were standing straight up in defiance along the cowlick!*

*As my blood began to boil, I opened my mouth to give an angry lecture. I needed no rehearsal for this speech! As I drew a deep breath that would sustain the volume and intensity my emotions required, I heard a small, repentant voice say, "I just don't understand it, Mom. My feet just won't do what my mind says it wants to."*

PART THREE

# When You Take a Wrong Turn

ELEVEN

# The Baby-Sitter's Lesson

DAD ALWAYS SAID the oldest one in the house at any given time was the boss. I took my position and authority seriously.

One day I was baby-sitting my four younger sisters and brother while Mother and Dad were out making church-related calls. I painstakingly made lunch for everyone and then stood at the bottom of the big open staircase in the parsonage and yelled, "Come and get it! Lunch is ready!"

No clatter of feet on the stairs, no sign of movement or acknowledgment of my announcement. Weren't they hungry? Where were they?

Then I heard giggles and happy squeals from one of the bedrooms. My sisters and brother had turned one of the big double beds into a trampoline and were jumping up and down on it. They were ignoring me! They were having so much fun they were pretending not to hear me. My temper flared. Again I yelled. "Lunch is ready! Come downstairs right now!"

Still no response. The giggles grew louder, which added fuel to my anger.

I bellowed, "LUNCH IS ON THE TABLE! YOU ARE STRICTLY FORBIDDEN TO JUMP ON THE BEDS! I AM THE RULER OVER YOU, AND I

COMMAND YOU TO COME DOWNSTAIRS AND EAT THIS FOOD!"

At that moment, they obediently jumped off the bed—and I felt in charge once again. I could hear them walking toward the stairs. They were whispering to each other when they suddenly gathered in a semicircle at the top of the stairs, pointed their bony little fingers in my direction, and taunted in unison, *"She is the RULER over us! She COMMANDS us to come downstairs and eat our food!"*

I've never forgotten the embarrassment, or the lesson. *Having* authority over people and circumstances and *thinking* you have authority are two totally different things. Position *does* bring authority. But when in authority, you need to choose the right words—or they come back to haunt you!

***Watch your words and hold your tongue;***
***you'll save yourself a lot of grief.***

Proverbs 21:23, MSG

***The right word at the right time***
***is like a custom-made piece of jewelry.***

Proverbs 25:11, MSG

TWELVE

# Is Anybody Home?

RECENTLY, I HAD a long-overdue heart-to-heart talk with my brother, Ben. There was passion in his voice. Regret. Release. Renewed commitment to God. He related several incidents that made him reevaluate his life, his marriage, and his commitment to family. One event involving his son, Zachary, reminds me that God often uses our children to pierce our hearts with poignant truth. But I'll let him tell the story.

> "By the time children are five, their parents will have done at least half of all that can ever be done to determine the children's future faith."
>
> —RANDOLPH MILLER, *Quotable Quotes*

The last few years I'd been working long hours. A typical office day started at 6:00 A.M., and I was lucky to make it home by 7:00 or 8:00 P.M. I knew I wasn't spending much time with Cathy and the kids, but I had my work and they had each other. Cathy is a great mother, and she was managing the family very well. When I finally made it home, I'd drop into a chair and turn on the television, or I would just sit. I rationalized that I needed it; I worked hard for it. If everyone would just leave me alone for a few minutes, I would be just fine.

In the back of my mind I knew the kids wanted me to play with them and Cathy needed me to talk to her. *But I just wanted to be left alone*. I put them off with a long string of excuses. Each day I used a different reason for not spending time with them.

"Not right now. . . ."

"Daddy needs to rest. . . ."

"In a minute. . . ."

"Go ahead—I'll be right there. . . ."

"Let's talk about it tomorrow. . . ."

Sometimes, when I was totally exhausted, I just said, "No!"

I soon discovered the easiest way to tune them out was to stare at the television in a zombielike fashion and just *not listen to them*. Sometimes I wasn't even watching a program. I had just mentally zoned out.

One day while I was in one of those catatonic states, I didn't hear Zachary ask me to play. I didn't pay him any attention when he got tired of asking and shortened his plea to just "Dad" and then started shouting, "Dad! Dad! Dad! *Dad!* DAD! *DAD!*" I didn't notice when he came around to the side of my chair and started pulling on my sleeve as he continued with his intense supplication.

Exasperated, he climbed onto the large arm of my overstuffed chair. Initially, I ignored my precious son as he leaned over in front of me, moving his small frustrated face so that his nose was almost touching mine.

Zachary finally got my attention when he placed his head down horizontally—directly in front of my face. At that moment he called out in a loud, clear voice, "HELLO! DAD! IS ANYBODY HOME? ARE YOU IN THERE?"

I laughed and swooped him up in my arms and tickled

him. It seemed humorous at the time. But it wasn't until much later when I was sharing this "funny" story with a friend that I realized how sad the situation was. My wife was hurting. My children were hurting. And my relationship with God was strained.

God used Zachary to remind me of how often I respond to God in the same way. I tune Him out because I'm tired. I give the same excuses, "Not now . . . maybe later. . . ." He patiently knocks on the door of my heart, persistently trying to get my attention. *Is anybody home?*

***"The people I love, I call to account—***
***prod and correct and guide so that they'll***
***live at their best. . . .***

***"Look at me. I stand at the door. I knock.***
***If you hear me call and open the door,***
***I'll come right in and sit down***
***to supper with you."***

Revelation 3:19-20, MSG

THIRTEEN

# The Policeman and the Purse

MY SISTER JENNIE AND I live about four hours apart on opposite sides of Michigan, so the telephone is a major link in our frequent communications. One day she called with a wild tale.

Late one morning she was driving home from her accountant's office. She had stayed up for hours the night before, gathering information, checking her totals for accuracy, and making sure her papers were in order. The accountant pored over the columns of numbers and announced that Jennie's math was correct, all tax information was recorded properly, and her records were so perfect they could pass an IRS investigation.

As she got into her car, she felt exuberant. The sun was shining, and since she was driving on a long, isolated stretch of country road, she started singing at the top of her lungs, *"I'm so glad I'm a part of the family of God."*[1] At that moment she drove over the crest of a hill and saw a police car coming toward her with the red light flashing.

Groaning, she lifted her foot from the accelerator. After the police car whizzed past, she saw it make a sharp U-turn in her rear-view mirror. Her heart sank as she realized she was about to be nabbed.

With hands trembling, she steered toward the shoulder of the road and rolled down the window to face the Oceana County Sheriff's deputy. With a grave face, he said, "May I see your license, registration, and proof of insurance, please?"

My sister usually carries a *big* purse that she fills with everything she might ever need while away from home: her identification, money, credit cards, breath fresheners, Tylenol, two or three shades of fingernail polish, lipstick, grocery store coupons, pencils, pens, business cards, keys, tissues (new and used), receipts (to be sorted later), postage stamps, Scotch tape, and a sewing kit. The list could go on, but you get the idea! She looked up at the officer with embarrassment and spoke.

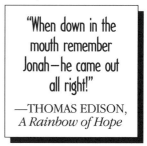

"When down in the mouth remember Jonah—he came out all right!"

—THOMAS EDISON, *A Rainbow of Hope*

"Yes, sir. Here's my license. Officer, I'll have to dig for the rest."

The policeman looked at her driver's license and soberly responded. "Jennie Dimkoff from Fremont, Michigan. Well, Jennie Dimkoff, do you know just how fast you were going?"

"I'm not exactly sure, sir, but I have an awful feeling you're going to tell me."

"I clocked you at seventy-two miles per hour. Ma'am, would you like to tell me why you were in such a hurry this morning?"

Jennie sighed. After a brief pause, she solemnly looked up and spoke.

"I have absolutely no excuse, officer. You see, I'm on my way home from a meeting with my accountant. It felt so good to have all that paperwork taken care of that I was just driving along enjoying the beauty of the sunshine, singing out loud at the top of my lungs. I simply didn't consider how fast I was going. I have no excuse, sir."

The officer seemed visibly surprised.

"I see," he mumbled. "Do you have your registration and proof of insurance?"

Jennie interrupted her frantic "tunneling operation" through the big purse and checked the glove compartment for the registration. Nothing. Breaking out in a cold sweat, she returned to the purse, fully aware that the police officer had a bird's-eye view of her "personal rattrap." After another humiliating couple of minutes, she produced a frayed piece of paper from her wallet. She handed it to the policeman with a feeling of triumph, only to be informed that it was an old proof of insurance that had expired four years earlier.

Panicking, she searched again. Moments later, exasperated, she made eye contact with the officer and blurted out, "Well, did *you* see anything that looked like a registration certificate in this purse?"

The officer was not amused. He excused himself and went back to his patrol car and appeared to be talking on the radio. Jennie was convinced he was checking to see if she was driving a stolen car.

When he finally returned, she spoke first.

"I'm in big trouble, aren't I?"

He wasn't smiling and his voice was firm.

"You certainly are, Mrs. Dimkoff. Do you realize you've earned yourself *three* tickets today? One for speeding, one for driving without your registration, and another for having no proof of insurance!"

Sick to her stomach and on the verge of tears, Jennie was no longer able to look him in the eye. But when he spoke again, her embarrassment turned into amazement.

He said, "I don't know what's gotten into me today, because *you really do deserve those tickets*, but if you were feeling so great this morning that you were *singing* on your way home, I'm not going to ruin your whole day by writing up those tickets!"

He started walking back to the patrol car. As she watched him in her rear-view mirror, he halted and turned back in her direction. With a determined voice, he ordered, "And, lady, I want you to *clean out that purse!*"

***He doesn't treat us as our sins deserve,***
***nor pay us back in full for our wrongs.***
***As high as heaven is over the earth,***
***so strong is his love to those who fear him.***
***And as far as sunrise is from sunset,***
***he has separated us from our sins.***

Psalm 103:10-12, MSG

FOURTEEN

# The Happy Mohawk Canoe Trip

ONE SUMMER I was a counselor at a camp for delinquent girls. Maria, the daughter of a migrant worker, was in my cabin. She spoke very little English and stayed close beside me.

One sunny day our camp director suggested that we take our campers to the Happy Mohawk Canoe Livery. When we arrived, I told the camp director that since I had never been canoeing before, it might be wise for me to be in the last canoe so I could observe the others.

Shy Maria looked at me and said, "I can't swim. Can I be in your safe canoe?" I told her to hop in. We used our life preservers as seat cushions in the bottom of the canoe and started paddling down the river. It was more like a placid little stream, but it was challenging enough for my inexperience.

We managed our canoe just fine until we reached a fork in the middle of the river, and I saw that the canoes in my party were going down the right-hand side of the fork. I had no idea how to steer a canoe.

While Maria and I struggled to follow the others, we crashed into the embankment in the center of the river. The branches of a tree were arched over our canoe, and I looked up to see a long, slithery snake on a branch just above our heads. A veteran camp counselor, I had endured frogs in sleeping bags, spiders on cabin walls, mosquitoes, and fire ants, but snakes immobilize me.

But as I saw the desperate look in Maria's eyes, my maternal instinct rose to its highest level. I leaned over, grabbed one of the paddles, stood up, and swung. To this day I have no idea whether or not I actually hit the snake. In that split second the canoe went over, and within a few more seconds it was caught in the current and going downstream fast, followed by our life preservers and paddles.

Maria was several feet away from me, splashing her arms and yelling, "Help me! Help me! I can't swim!" She went under water.

I was kicking my feet, flailing my arms, desperately trying to get to my camper, but getting nowhere fast in the strong current.

Maria's head came up a second time as she screamed, "Please help me! I'm drowning!"

Panic was setting in. Her head went under. I looked to the right, saw two men coming in a canoe, and began to yell, "Help us! We're drowning! We're drowning!"

It seemed to take thirty minutes for the men to get to us, but it was probably more like thirty seconds. They finally arrived and paused for a brief moment to watch me continue to splash frantically. One man calmly asked, "Hey, lady, why don't you just stand up?"

When I quit struggling and stood up, I found out I was in three feet of water. When Maria came up for what appeared to be her last breath on this earth and saw me standing, she stood up and was saved, too.

I swallowed my pride and said, "Thank you very much." I had almost drowned in three feet of water—and yet the ground was beneath my feet the whole time!

This world is full of people who are spiritually drowning, yet struggling hard to earn God's favor. Their flailing efforts are fruitless. But God offers sure footing—if they will just ask.

*Now God has us where he wants us. . . .*
*Saving is all his idea, and all his work.*
*All we do is trust him enough to let him do it.*
*It's God's gift from start to finish! We don't play the*
*major role. If we did, we'd probably*
*go around bragging that we'd done the whole*
*thing! No, we neither make nor save ourselves.*
*God does both the making and saving.*

Ephesians 2:7-10, MSG

FIFTEEN

# No Place to Hide

MY HUSBAND'S FATHER was a plumber for the Grand Trunk Railroad, and they lived in a house right next to the railroad tracks. As a child Gene spent hours watching the trains go by. He enthusiastically waved at the engineers, and they often waved back.

Frequently, empty boxcars were left on the side tracks until they were needed. The cars measured eighteen feet in height and fifty feet in length, with an access ladder on the end leading to a large hand brake at the top. A grated walkway extended down the full length of the top of each boxcar.

With dangerous tracks so close to the house, Gene's dad had forcefully outlined several rules for his sons: "I don't ever want to catch you boys on those tracks! And I don't ever want to find you anywhere near those boxcars! *Do you understand me?*" They understood, and he didn't have to elaborate on the punishment; Gene and his two brothers *knew* the penalty—Dad's belt! It was thick and black and long, and each of them had felt it before.

Occasionally they pleaded, "But all our friends play on the tracks, and we'd be careful!" His dad was unrelenting with good reason. Every few years someone who worked on the trains had an accident, and it wasn't just a bump or a bruise—it was a lost leg or an arm or a hand. One of his father's closest friends had lost both legs in a freak accident involving those big, unwieldy boxcars. His threatening warning was spoken because of his love for his boys.

One summer some of the neighbor kids came by the house and wanted to play tag on the boxcars. This was great fun. They would race up the ladder on one end, run across the grating at the top, and jump from one car to the next. It seemed safe enough—and no one ever got hurt. Well, practically no one!

That afternoon Gene knew his mom and dad were at work. His father's job was on the other side of town. Gene was convinced his father couldn't see him or ever find out, so he agreed to join his friends. They chose someone to be "it" and took off for the boxcars. They ran up the ladders and raced as fast as they dared down the grated walkways, leaping from one boxcar to the next like wild monkeys. The potential danger only made their adrenaline flow faster. It was a rush like no other. What fun!

For about twenty minutes they were having a great time. Gene was sprinting across the top of one of the cars and happened to look out at the road that ran near the side tracks where they were playing. With horror he saw his father's truck going by.

His dad's eyes locked onto his, and Gene knew he was in trouble! He raced to the end of the boxcar and scrambled down the ladder. When he hit the ground, he tore off like mad for the house.

His father pulled his truck to the side of the road, jumped out, and began running for the house, too. He was pulling off his belt at the same time. Gene beat him to the porch and began begging for mercy. Clutching the back of his pants, he pleaded, "Dad, I promise I'll *never* climb on the boxcars again! I promise I'll *never* spill my milk again! I promise I will *never* sass Mom again for the rest of my life!"

But it was too late—he'd been caught! In spite of his pleading and begging, he was punished. And the lesson was learned. Disobedience has a penalty.

***Is there anyplace I can go to avoid your Spirit?***
***to be out of your sight?***
***If I climb to the sky, you're there!***
***If I go underground, you're there!***
***If I flew on morning's wings***
***to the far western horizon,***
***You'd find me in a minute—***
***you're already there waiting!***

Psalm 139:7-10, MSG

SIXTEEN

# The Man on the Bicycle

IT HAD BEEN QUITE A WHILE since I'd spent any amount of time on the campus of an institution of higher learning. The signs in the dormitory I was staying in were typical: Keep This Door Closed; Turn Lights Out to Conserve Electricity. There were special signs in the parking lot, too: Student Parking, Permit Required. Unauthorized Vehicles Will Be Towed Away at Owner's Expense.

For the first three days of the conference there were two empty parking spaces right in front of my dormitory window. My car was parked in a lot more than a block away. Thinking about all of the heavy luggage I needed to load after the conference, I rationalized that the signs in the parking places probably only applied to the school year. This was August. I promptly moved my car into one of the restricted parking spaces.

The next morning I spoke to a spirited group of women on "The Joy of Submitting to God's Authority in Our Lives." The group was attentive and responsive.

My heart was singing as I went back to my dorm room to drop off my Bible and briefcase before getting lunch. Glancing out the window, I realized *something* was missing: my car was no longer in the parking place where I had left it.

I was mortified. *How could I go to the director of this conference and admit that right after speaking on submitting to God's authority, I had gotten caught not submitting to man's authority?*

I meekly made my way to the back of the building and found a maintenance man. "Can you tell me where cars are taken when they are towed away from the college?"

"They're taken to Dick's Towing Service." With a sweeping gesture, he continued, "It's just a few blocks in that direction." The college employee was obviously used to the question. I had to speak again at 2:15 P.M., but I realized if I hurried I could get my car back and avoid any possible embarrassment connected with this incident. I quickly began walking in the direction the man had pointed. Carloads of women were driving by waving and smiling at their speaker. I waved and smiled back, as if nothing was wrong.

Several blocks later, I realized I was lost. Observing an old man on a bicycle in the middle of the street, I called out, "Sir, do you know where Dick's Towing Service is located?" He stopped and said he *did* know where the towing service was located. The man wheeled his bike in my direction. He told me he was a retired schoolteacher, and we chatted briefly about education. He was riding an oversized bicycle with some extra seat room on it, and he politely said, "Lady, why don't you hop on? I'll have you there in a minute."

My feet were killing me. I was in a hurry. Glancing at my watch, I thought, *How good of God to provide me with this instant transportation from such a kind old gentleman.* I thanked him and hopped on.

Half a block later he turned down a dark alley, and I realized we were *not* in the business district. The man was breathing heavily—and I was praying it was because I was too heavy to pedal. I thought, *If he knows how frightened I am, I'll be in serious trouble.* With all the authority I could muster, I mumbled, "I-I-I think we're both lost. Why don't you just drop me off and I'll go back to the college and have someone drive me to the towing service."

He immediately responded, "Why don't I take you back to my place, and you can make a phone call?"

As we came to the next crosswalk, I literally leaped off the bicycle. He turned the bike toward me and said, "Couldn't you just give me *one* little kiss?"

I was so shocked I answered him, "No, sir! I couldn't even think of it!" I began to run as fast as my high heels would click—and he pedaled right beside me.

One more time, he shouted in my direction: "Couldn't you just give me *one* little kiss?"

There was no one else visible in the street. I saw a nearby house with the screen door closed and the main door open, indicating someone might be inside. I raced up on the porch and pressed on the doorbell with one hand while I knocked with the other hand. The man was waiting for me in the street.

An older woman came to the door. I thought if she knew the man in front of her house was after me, she'd be so frightened she wouldn't let me in. Talking as fast as I could spit the words out, I said, "Ma'am, I'm speaking at the college this week and my car was towed away. It's been taken to Dick's Towing Service. I'm having trouble locating the towing service, and I wonder if I could use your telephone and find out where I'm supposed to be."

She paused a moment, evaluating the woman on her porch with the unusual story. After hesitating, her mouth broadened into a big grin and she said, "You come right in here."

Taking me to her kitchen, she lifted the telephone receiver and placed a call to the towing service. After obtaining directions, she looked up and said, "I'll drive you to the spot where your car has been taken." We left out her back door (an exit not visible from the front of the house) and departed in her car through an alley behind the main street.

Within a short time I once again held the keys to my confiscated car. I thanked my rescuer and returned to the college in time for the 2:15 P.M. speaking assignment.

Later, when I had time to consider the terrifying what-ifs of my eventful day, I thought about the questions that trouble us in the middle of life.

Did my sin of parking in a prohibited spot result in jeopardizing my safety?

Why did I thank God for providing "instant transportation" when I made such an unwise choice?

Why do some women wind up being raped or even killed for doing no more than I did that day—accepting a ride from a stranger?

Why was I spared from so much pain and others aren't?

*We don't yet see things clearly.*
*We're squinting in a fog, peering through a mist.*
*But it won't be long before the weather clears*
*and the sun shines bright! We'll see it all then,*
*see it all as clearly as God sees us,*
*knowing him directly just as he knows us!*

*But for right now, until that completeness,*
*we have three things to do to lead us*
*toward that consummation:*
*Trust steadily in God, hope unswervingly,*
*love extravagantly. And the best of the three*
*is love.*

1 Corinthians 13:12-13, MSG

SEVENTEEN

# The Mouth That Roared

MARY WADDLED up to the front of the sanctuary after my Bible study lecture. I found myself wondering if she would be stopping by the hospital to deliver her baby on the way home from the church.

"Carol, do you have time to talk?" she asked.

"Sure, I'd love to. How are you feeling?"

"Pregnant—*very pregnant*."

I knew this had been an unexpected and difficult pregnancy for her. She had two preschoolers at home already, and the prospect of a newborn on top of her current pressures seemed a bit overwhelming. We took seats on the front pew.

> DEFINITION
> Nah-Nahs: negative verbal and nonverbal responses to the people we love when we are stressed out, under pressure, and exhausted.

She blurted out, "Do you know what God's been teaching me through our Bible study this year?"

"What's that?" I asked, curious to know if anything I had been saying was making a difference in somebody's life.

"He's been telling me that I need to get rid of the

Nah-Nahs," she said matter-of-factly.

"What did you say?" I queried. She was using a phrase that wasn't in my vocabulary, and I doubted that it was in the dictionary.

She continued. "You know, I'm big and fat and pregnant and uncomfortable and grouchy, and I get up in the morning feeling so-o-o-o terrible and I go 'Nah-Nah! When is this baby going to be born and give me back my former self?' I go into my children's room in the morning and trip over their toys and messes and dirty clothes and I go, 'Nah-Nah! This place looks like a pigsty. It's time to get up and clean this room up.'"

She went on. "I gripe through their breakfast and complain while I make their peanut butter and jelly sandwiches for lunch. I Nah-Nah when my back hurts and yell at those kids for being normal two- and three-year-olds. When John comes home, I put leftovers on the table.

"He says, 'Oh, leftovers *again?*'

"And I respond, 'Nah-Nah—if you don't like them, you can cook for yourself!'"

Her hands were folded over the top of her gigantic belly. I wondered how she could keep breathing so easily with such a bundle to carry around. There were tears in her eyes as her voice softened. "As I was doing my Bible study assignment this week, I realized that I am a *terrible* person to live with. I wake up in the morning Nah-Nahing to my kids, I go through my day Nah-Nahing when I make meals, clean up the house, do laundry, and when I greet my husband. *I don't even like living with myself anymore!*"

Mary didn't need counseling. She needed a listening ear. I nodded to indicate I certainly understood where she was coming from. She went on. "After I finished my Bible study, I got down on my knees beside the bed—and I'm so pregnant I can hardly assume that position—and I lifted my open hands to the Lord and prayed, 'Lord, You take the Nah-Nahs. I do not want to be a woman with negative words on my tongue day and night. I don't want my children to leave home someday thinking how happy they are to get away from such a whining, complaining mother. I don't want my husband to dread coming home.

"'I want to be a woman with praise and affirmation on her lips. It's my desire to have my children remember that I celebrated their accomplishments and applauded their efforts. Help me to be a mother who reflects joy, peace, and serenity—instead of disapproval, irritation, and criticism. Put a guard on my tongue. Fill my mouth with tributes to You and to those I love.'"

That day Mary understood a principle that takes some of us years to learn.

***Watch the way you talk. . . .***
***Say only what helps, each word a gift.***

***Don't grieve God. Don't break his heart. His Holy Spirit, moving and breathing in you, is the most intimate part of your life, making you fit for himself. Don't take such a gift for granted.***

***Make a clean break with all cutting, backbiting, profane talk. Be gentle with one another, sensitive. Forgive one another as quickly and thoroughly as God in Christ forgave you.***

Ephesians 4:29-32, MSG

*When our son was five years old,
Gene and I had numerous conversations
in which we expressed our dismay that
three miles from our front door,
at the main corner where cars turn toward
our subdivision, a Cinema Blue movie
theater was being built. The theater ran
advertisements in our local paper
promoting live girlie shows and
triple-X-rated movies.*

*One day after the theater opened,
our family drove by it and saw its colorful,
flashing lights and full parking lot.
Suddenly, J.P. put his hands on his hips,
looked disdainfully out the car window
toward the theater, shook his head back
and forth, and with an "adult" tone said,
"Boy, a lot of people sure must
love the Devil!"*

PART FOUR

# When God Turns Tragedy to Triumph

EIGHTEEN

# Lord, It's Father's Day

FOR MORE THAN A DECADE, Gene worked for an insurance company that employed a lot of Christians. The conventions were more like spiritual renewal conferences than motivational sales meetings. On one trip to the West Coast, we were invited to the home of Harley and Johnnie (her real name) Sowell. Because of the bond we shared as believers, the evening was full of laughter and Christian camaraderie. As the conversation moved to our spiritual journeys and what we had learned about God, Harley told us the following story about a fishing trip he took with his sons on Father's Day weekend of 1964.

---

It was almost dark on Friday evening when my two sons and I, along with my good friend Ollie and his son, were ready to leave on a fishing trip to the high Sierra mountains. Tim, my older son, was sixteen years old and sat with Ollie and me in the front seat of the truck. My son Stephen and Ollie's son, Gary, were both thirteen. They sat in the back with all of the gear we needed for a weekend of camping.

When we reached Huntington Lake, we left the main

road and headed for Hoffman Meadows, where we were going to set up the base camp. From there we planned to hike into the canyon in order to fish the South Fork of the San Joaquin River.

Around the next bend our headlights revealed a hiker who needed a ride. We offered assistance and agreed to take him as far as we could. The bearded stranger rode with the boys in the back of the truck. Stephen and Gary were tucked into their sleeping bags to get some protection from the cold. They were too timid to talk to the stranger, but whispered that he looked exactly like pictures they had seen of Jesus. Stephen and Gary were enjoying every minute of this great adventure. After dropping the stranger off, we set up our base camp and fell asleep, exhausted.

We arose with the sun the next morning. After a hearty breakfast, we started our descent into the canyon. Gary and Stephen were like a couple of young colts, feeling their early morning oats.

Ollie stopped our single-file procession to remind the boys that we were in rattlesnake country and that they would be well advised to watch where they were walking. Two hundred yards later Ollie stepped right next to a coiled rattler. Gary and Stephen, who were mocking Ollie's walk by stepping in each of his footprints, were equally close to the danger of the coiled snake. Tim was next in line, and he almost knocked me over as he instinctively reversed his direction while simultaneously yelling, "SNAKE!"

Within seconds, we realized the coolness of the early morning hour had rendered the snake harmless and prevented him from striking. We were out of danger—or so we thought. Sometimes obvious danger can be rendered harmless, and what appears to be serene can be perilous.

It was about 9:00 A.M. when we reached the river and could start fishing. We planned to go downstream. All trout fishermen try to be the first one to find the best spot along the river. Leapfrogging around each other is a common occurrence—and part of the sport! That day was no exception. We were strung out along a quiet section of this picturesque river. Everyone was catching fish and enjoying the exquisite beauty of God's majestic creation.

From their earliest days of fishing, I had instructed my boys about what to do if we ever got separated. I told them to stay near the water until I found them. The San Joaquin River often appears quiet on the surface, but there are dangerous rapids and strong subterranean currents in unexpected places. That day I was deliberately bringing up the rear, assuming that all were ahead of me as they fished downstream.

At about noon all of us met together at a rather large pool—all except Stephen. Tim said the last time he saw his brother he was on a large rock at the lower end of this same pool. We agreed that Ollie would investigate downstream and I would cover upstream and that we would meet back at the pool after our search.

We all returned with nothing to report. As we stood on the rocks at the lower end of the pool, we suddenly saw the tip of Stephen's fishing pole sticking up out of the rocks. While we could cross the river by walking on a series of rocks that were just above water level, the stream next to the big rock where Stephen was last seen was about five feet deep. I felt a knot forming in the pit of my stomach.

With dread, I suggested that I hold onto Tim and have him search in the deep water next to the big rock. Ollie immediately countered my suggestion by reminding me that Stephen was an excellent swimmer. He wisely stated that we should not risk anyone else. The knot in my stomach tightened.

After hours of calling his name and searching up and down the river's edge, I was still clinging desperately to the hope that he was lost and would soon return. We decided I would spend the night there while Ollie, Gary, and Tim went for help. I built a large fire to keep warm and to ward off the mountain lions. I tried to stay awake, but when exhaustion overcame me and I dozed off, I heard Stephen calling out to me. Lurching to a standing position, I rushed out into the night, only to find I was dreaming. Again and again I called out his name in the stillness of the night, but there was no answer.

During the next few hours, I prayed that Stephen would see the fire and come back. I looked into the star-studded blue sky. Moments later I sensed God speaking to my troubled heart. "You may be called upon to give up your son involuntarily. But remember that I voluntarily gave My Son so whoever would believe in Him would have eternal life." Somehow, that cold and lonely place became a sanctuary as I waited in those early morning hours. I sensed the supernatural presence of God on that Father's Day morning. I know now that He was preparing me for what the next few hours would reveal.

At eight o'clock the next morning Ollie and Tim returned with a rescue team from the Fresno County Sheriff's Department, along with a contingent of young men from our church. Within the next hour, the rescue team found the lifeless body of Stephen trapped under water at the base of the big rock. He had been wedged face down, far beneath the surface, by the pressure of a strong current entering a subterranean cavity. No one would have suspected the life-threatening danger below when the surface of the water appeared to be so peaceful.

It took several hours of hiking to get back out of the canyon. My heart ached as I accompanied the rescue workers who were carrying the lifeless form of my thirteen-year-old son.

But slowly, God began to show us reasons for hope. Stephen had accepted Christ as his Savior at an early age, and in spite of our heartbreaking loss, we knew he was safe in the arms of Jesus. Stephen's best friend was from an unchurched home, and he took his friend's death very hard. I went to him and explained that, while we, too, were grieving deeply over the loss of our son, it was not like people who have no hope. I explained that Stephen is with Jesus and we will see him again. As a direct result of Stephen's death, this young man was challenged with the gospel message and accepted Christ as his personal Savior. Today he is in the ministry.

As my thoughts return to the evening I first heard this story, I remember Harley's description of his conversation with God as he waited alone beside the pool on that desolate night in the high Sierras.

"Lord, it's Father's Day. Is this some kind of a joke? I've always said You can take anything from me, but don't take my children. . . . It came to me in the middle of those dark hours that my heavenly Father *did* understand."

***"This is how much God loved the world:<br>He gave his Son, his one and only Son.<br>And this is why: so that no one need be destroyed;<br>by believing in him, anyone can have a whole<br>and lasting life."***

John 3:16, MSG

NINETEEN

# At Gunpoint in the Dress Shop

SEVERAL YEARS AGO I was researching the topic of God's covenant relationship with His people. During my study, I watched a videotape of one of Kay Arthur's Bible study messages from Precept Ministries in Chattanooga, Tennessee. One of her illustrations gripped my heart as I was reminded of the power we have over the Enemy.

Kay was teaching on Joshua 1:1-9. She emphasized the strength of God's words to Joshua as he took over the leadership of the children of Israel: "Have I not commanded you? Be strong and courageous. Do not be terrified; do not be discouraged, for the LORD your God will be with you wherever you go" (verse 9).

As she ended her message, Kay spoke with great authority. "We don't have to be afraid of anyone or anything. If God is before us, who can be against us?" At the conclusion of her challenge, she looked at the crowd, and with an upward gesture, she shouted, "CHARGE!"

Not long after hearing this message, Carol, a woman from the audience, went to a downtown dress shop to purchase a new outfit for a shower she was planning to attend. It was a warm Saturday afternoon, and she was glancing in the mirror at the first dress she tried on.

At that moment the curtains opened and a tall man stood in the doorway. She was startled. Moments earlier he had taken money from the store's cash register and made the two salesclerks remove their clothes and lie under the counter. He then walked into the dressing room where Carol was standing. He had a knife in one hand and a gun in the other. Later it was discovered that he had previously been convicted of second-degree murder.

He spoke distinctly to Carol. "Take all your clothes off and lie down on the floor."

Calmly, she looked at him with steady eye contact and said, "No, I will not."

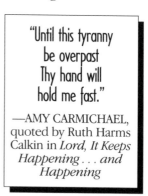

> "Until this tyranny
> be overpast
> Thy hand will
> hold me fast."
>
> —AMY CARMICHAEL, quoted by Ruth Harms Calkin in *Lord, It Keeps Happening . . . and Happening*

His eyes were filled with anger, hatred, and fear, as he pushed her to the floor and kicked her several times. As she struggled to get up, he held a knife to her face and said, "Either you do what I say or I'll kill you."

She calmly spoke again. *"I command you in the name of the Lord Jesus Christ to leave me alone!"*

Immediately the man's hand, holding the knife, dropped to his side. His look of anger and hatred changed to bewilderment as he backed out of the dressing room and walked out of the store. Later, he was apprehended by the police. After a trial, he was sent to prison.

Almost a year had passed when Carol received a letter from the prisoner.

Dear Sister in Christ,

I want you to know that the chain of events that took place in that dress shop on Saturday, February 26, 1977, was something that started me on a course that has changed my entire life.

Before that day in 1977, and even until just recently, I had been a sinner all of my thirty-five years of life. I have done nothing good for myself except rob many people of their hard-earned money. I have broken into many people's homes and businesses. I had used just about every type of drug and narcotic I could buy or steal.

At that time, I had no feelings or sympathy for anything or anyone. I was out to get what I could from whom I could, regardless of who I hurt or how much I hurt them.

Because of my education, which was and is not very much, and because I had no special skills, I was unable to even get a worthwhile job (it was no excuse for me to do the wrong thing). Even then, I knew that unless something drastic happened, my life was on a dead-end course.

On Saturday, February 26, 1977, when I was attempting to rob that dress shop, you made a statement to me that literally, physically sent chills down my back. You said, "In the name of Jesus Christ, I command you to leave me alone." At that very moment I felt the presence of something very strong and powerful. My physical being was unable to function temporarily.

For months on end, after the incident, I would lay awake at night and would not be able to sleep for thinking of the statement you made to me while looking me right in my eyes, and the "feeling" that came over me at that time. At times I would even get cold chills thinking of it.

After I escaped from jail last August, my life was so messed up and I had so little hope for the future. I took a loaded pistol and almost took my own life. After I was recaptured, I was placed in an isolation cell by myself. Nothing was in that cell except a small New Testament, and once again I would find myself thinking of you and that statement you made to me, and also the feeling I had at that time. I don't remember what day or night it was, but I started to read that New Testament.

In the second week of January of this year, I was saved by the Lord and dedicated the remainder of my life to Jesus Christ to do with as He sees fit.

I attend church services every week here at the jail and have given my testimony many times. As you know, it is very, very hard when you are trying to live a Christian life in a jail or a prison. I have been talked about, scorned, and made fun of because I have confessed the Lord Jesus Christ as my personal Savior. I have stood firm in my belief, and now many people here in jail, the prisoners and guards alike, are actually surprised and shocked that I have become a Christian. I realize that I may never again be a free man for the rest of my life in a physical sense, but my soul will forever be free.

That statement you made to me will be a living testament to anyone I come into contact with for the rest of my life. Please give your entire family my sincere regards, and I pray that God will continue to bless and keep you all under His loving care. Again, I thank you, Mrs. Clark, for opening my eyes, and I thank God for saving a sinner like me.

Sincerely,
Your Brother in Christ

***Be prepared. You're up against far more***
***than you can handle on your own.***
***Take all the help you can get,***
***every weapon God has issued,***
***so that when it's all over but the shouting***

*you'll still be on your feet. Truth, righteousness, peace, faith, and salvation are more than words. Learn how to apply them. You'll need them throughout your life. God's Word is an* indispensable *weapon. In the same way, prayer is essential in this ongoing warfare. Pray hard and long. . . . Keep your eyes open.*

Ephesians 6:12-18, MSG

TWENTY

# Sid's Homegoing

THE SUN WAS GLISTENING on the jagged, rocky cliffs of Yosemite National Park. All of God's creation echoed the greatness of His almighty power. Awestruck, my husband, Gene, and I weaved around the curvy canyon road with our new friends, Vern and Betty Ens. I wanted to freeze the emotion of that moment, along with the regal scene before me—a majestic postcard of glorious color, depth, and texture.

As the day of sightseeing progressed, our conversation became more intimate. Vern and Betty lived in Fresno, California. We had known them casually through the insurance business Vern and Gene worked for; however, this relaxing trip through Yosemite provided an opportunity to get better acquainted. They were "my kind of people." I loved their zest for life and their enthusiasm about discussing spiritual issues. During that trip they shared a story that has been one of the most significant tools God has used to help me develop an eternal perspective.

Vern and Betty had purchased a parcel of land up in the mountains. On Saturdays Vern took their two teenage boys to the property, where they were constructing a little cabin. One one of those Saturdays, Sid, age seventeen, wasn't feeling well. Later that week, Betty took him to the doctor for tests.

One week later, as Betty was finishing up a Bible study in her home, the phone rang. It was the doctor. He said, "Betty, I'm sorry to have to tell you this news. The tests have come back and Sid has cancer. He's young. We think we've caught it in time, but you need to bring him in right away so we can begin treatment."

Sid was a dynamic young man with so much ahead of him. He had good grades, a girlfriend, and a heart for the Lord. Treatment began. Sid went through chemotherapy, followed by radiation treatments. For a while his cancer was in remission. Then the tumors returned with a vengeance.

The doctor spoke to Vern and Betty about the possibility of trying a new, experimental treatment. When they asked Sid if he wanted to move forward with this idea, he looked up and said, "Mom and Dad, since I was young, you've always made decisions that you thought were the best for me. Right now, because of the pain and discomfort involved, I might be tempted to make the wrong choice. I'd like the two of you to get all the facts and make this decision."

They proceeded with the experimental treatment over the next few months, and Sid taught his parents a great lesson in trusting God. In spite of the physical discomfort he experienced during the treatments, he believed his parents were making the best decision for him. Vern said, "The trust Sid placed in us was the kind of trust God asks us to place in Him."

Within a few months, tests revealed that the experimental treatment was not producing the desired results. The cancer was progressing rapidly. Sid's condition was terminal.

We continued on our trip through the canyon, and Vern said, "I'll never forget the day, on Sid's nineteenth birthday, two years after this disease was first diagnosed, I carried him back through the doors of the hospital I had carried him out of nineteen years earlier."

Within a short time, the doctor came to Vern and Betty and said, "We've done everything we can for Sid. It's up to you, if you'd like to take him home for the time he has left."

They *did* bring Sid home. Vern and Betty shared the major responsibilities of caring for their precious son. Vern began wearing a pager on his belt, so Betty could contact him instantly while he was working.

> "Joy is a process, a journey—often muffled, sometimes detoured; a mystery in which we participate, not a product we can grasp. . . . Growth and joy are inhibited when we say 'if only,' enhanced when we realize that failures and difficulties are not only a critical part of the process, but are our very opportunities to grow."
>
> —TIM HANSEL, *You Gotta Keep Dancin'*

Two weeks after they brought Sid back home, Vern was across town for a business appointment. The pager went off and Vern knew Betty needed him. He called home and she said, "Honey, it's time. You need to come home right away."

In Fresno traffic is usually bumper-to-bumper, but that day it was as if God made a path for his car. Vern made it home in record time.

Sid had lost all bowel and bladder control—but not his sense of humor. Although he was in a weakened condition, as his dad came in the door, he looked up, smiled, and said, "You're just in time, Dad; I've made another mess."

They lovingly bathed their boy, clothed him, and propped him up in a comfortable position. Then they read Scripture, sang songs, prayed, and hugged.

Vern began to speak as he tenderly stroked his son's shoulder: "You know, Son, when the company sends me on a trip, I often don't get excited about the destination until my bags are packed. But when my suitcases are packed and

I board that plane, I get excited about where I'm going." He paused thoughtfully. "Son, you're going on a trip soon."

Sid smiled as he spoke. "I know, Dad. I'm going to see Jesus face to face. I'm going to be free of pain for the first time in so long. I'll get a new body. I'm really looking forward to going."

Vern's eyes were filling with tears as he responded. "When that time comes, Son, don't wait for us. This life is very short and we'll be there before you know it. Just lift your arms to Jesus and He'll pull you through to the other side."

Within a few minutes the most radiant smile came over Sid's face, his hands moved in an upward direction, and it was just as if God Himself reached through time and space and ushered him into heaven.

I was weeping in the back seat of the car. My nonemotional husband was wiping tears too. Betty looked at us with confidence as she said, "Don't cry for us. It was the most victorious moment of our lives."

She described what happened next. "I leaned over and closed Sid's eyes. Then Vern and I got on our knees at that bedside, and we held the celebration prayer of Sid's entrance into glory!" Betty's voice rang out with victory as she spoke of Sid's homegoing.

***Friends, when life gets really difficult,***
***don't jump to the conclusion***
***that God isn't on the job.***
***Instead, be glad that you are in the very thick***
***of what Christ experienced.***
***This is a spiritual refining process,***
***with glory just around the corner.***

1 Peter 4:12-13, MSG

TWENTY-ONE

# Two Fathers

AFTER A TEN-MINUTE conversation with her, I was convinced Katherine's one goal in life was to live for something that had eternal value. She was *passionate* about God and about getting His work done on this earth.

Katherine exudes the maturity that comes only from suffering. The wisdom in her eyes defied age. Instead of offering pat answers, she asked discerning questions. She enjoyed the *journey* more than the *destination*. Her weathered faith had been shaken by fierce storms, including a tornado or two, and the victor's flag was still flying at the top of her mast. She gave me a sense of balance in a topsy-turvy world.

Her story, which follows, reminds me that no matter what my circumstances are, I still have the opportunity to *choose* how I will respond.

My husband abandoned me when our son, Johnny, was eleven years old. When John turned fourteen, he too decided to leave me and live with his father in a city about one hundred miles from the small town where I lived.

His father found it "inconvenient" to have a teenager underfoot, and without my knowledge John was left without a roof over his head. He began living with people he met on the street.

About eighteen months after John left, I received a phone call from a hospital in Calgary requesting my health insurance card number. Johnny had been admitted as a patient. I supplied them with the required information and said I'd be there as soon as possible. However, they told me not to come. They said, "Your son does not want to see you."

A short while later I learned that some "friends" had given him LSD as a joke. His reaction to the drug was so severe that he was kept in a restraint. I was told my son would be a mental vegetable.

I was devastated.

A young couple next door to me had been praying for John with me once a week. Fearful and trembling, I ran to their home and poured out the story of the phone call. They put their arms around me, invited me inside, and began to petition heaven on behalf of John. Finally, I stopped shaking and began to pray with them.

Over time, my relationship with my troubled son was restored and, miraculously, he fully recovered. He returned home and started school again. His heart was turned back to God, and he began attending every service and youth event at our church.

He began to care deeply for a beautiful young woman in our church whom he'd known since childhood. His heart was broken when the girl's father forbade them to date, saying, "You are just like your father!" He had implied to us and others that he did not want John ruining his daughter's life!

John was crushed. Later, he sobbed out his hurt as he cried, "Oh, Mom, am I *always* going to be compared with my father? Will I end up like Dad?"

My son was hurting. I knew he was in grave danger of turning his back on Christianity and everything connected with it. I lifted my heart to God and prayed for insight. "Lord, I have no husband. I need Your wisdom. My son is in pain. Help me to know what to do."

Almost instantly God gave me the words to say. I cradled my son in my arms and then held his face in my hands. "Johnny, you have two fathers. You must choose which one you will follow."

> "We do not find God's presence without first wading through His absence."
>
> —SUE MONK KIDD, *God's Joyful Surprise*

From that point on, something was different. I watched my heavenly Father faithfully lead my son, correct him, encourage him, and *father* him.

Today John is a successful businessman and is married to a precious Christian woman. He is the father of two little girls. This year he will receive his master of divinity degree, and he plans to leave the business world and go into the ministry.

His mind—once thought irreversibly damaged—is keen.

His heart—once broken—is full of compassion for the hurting.

His life—once seemingly useless—is a productive tool in God's hand.

***What marvelous love the Father has extended to us! Just look at it—we're called children of God! That's who we really are.***

1 John 3:1, MSG

*When J.P. was born, we were showered with baby gifts. Along with a great supply of diapers, sleepers, bottles, rattles, and other practical presents, we received a remarkable endowment of heirloom-quality blankets: handmade quilts, pink and blue afghans knitted by the hands of praying grandmothers, christening blankets trimmed in exquisite white lace, blankets with satin borders. J.P.'s nursery was well stocked with the most elegant baby blankets I had ever laid eyes on.*

*So, I was chagrined when it became obvious that J.P. had attached himself to the only truly ugly blanket in the pile. His favorite was an unattractive polyester "blue light special" from K-Mart. After a short time the graying white comforter developed unattractive balls of knotted material on the surface. The binding was shredding and dangled in a repulsive fashion at intermittent places along the perimeter.*

*The blanket embarrassed me. On numerous occasions, I hid the treasured rag and pulled out one of the exquisite blankets from the nursery closet. But all were rejected by my son—who had developed a loyalty to the unsightly item.*

*On one occasion, I rationalized that he was now old enough to be permanently severed from this unwholesome relationship with the tattered blanket. I removed it from his room while he was busy at play and replaced it with a bed covering of much finer quality. I carefully placed the polyester castoff in the kitchen wastebasket.*

*A bit later, I looked up from my work and found my son on a kitchen chair, clutching the discarded blanket to his face as tears streamed down his cheeks. He had just started praying with his own words, instead of using the memorized prayers we had taught him earlier.*

*With his head bowed over the precious blanket so recently saved from destruction, I heard him pray aloud: "Dear Jesus, You're just like a blanket, and I won't ever stop loving You."*

PART FIVE

# When You Don't Like God's Direction

TWENTY-TWO

# Can You See the Angels?

DR. DON DENMARK recently told me this remarkable story about a patient he treated.

Allen was twenty years old when I met him. He had terminal cancer and was very angry at God. His left leg had been amputated above the knee, and he was in tremendous pain. He knew he was dying, and he was afraid.

A friend of Allen's had approached me earlier and asked if I could provide care for him during his final days. I went to Allen and introduced myself as a physician. When I turned the conversation to spiritual things, Allen got increasingly angry.

He looked at me with rage in his eyes and said, "Don't you *dare* talk to me about God!"

I asked him why he was so upset, and he responded with sarcasm. "One of my *good-intentioned* neighbors came and told me the reason I have cancer is because of sin in my life."

But I was committed to care for him, to show him love, and to reach out to him. Each week I went to his home, talked to him, looked after his medical needs, and brought items to make his life more comfortable. When the opportunity presented itself, I continued to speak to him about Christ. My comments fell on deaf ears.

One morning while I was jogging, God very clearly told me, "You need to go and talk to Allen one more time, for today he's going to die."

Allen had been hospitalized two days earlier because the cancer had spread. His leg had formed a cavitating abscess and it was weeping severely. The only way we could manage the disease was in the hospital. I had promised him I would be honest with him about his condition. I went to the hospital, made rounds, and then entered Allen's room.

> "A visitor saw a nurse attending the sores of a leprosy patient. I would not do that for a million dollars, she said. The nurse answered, Neither would I, but I do it for Jesus for nothing."
>
> —CORRIE TEN BOOM, *Clippings from My Notebook*

There was a nurse in the room at the time, and I thought, *I can't talk to Allen about his spiritual need* now. *There's a nurse in this room. What would she think of me?*

I finished caring for Allen's medical needs, walked out of the room, and had taken two steps down the hall when a voice said, "You didn't do what I asked you to do. I asked you to go *one more time*." I turned around and no one was there. I don't know if that voice was an inner impression of the heart or a supernatural whisper in my ear—but there was no mistaking the source. It was the voice of God.

I turned and went back into the room and sat down at the side of the bed. "Allen, I said I'd be honest with you and I need to be. Today you're going to die."

His eyes lit up as he looked up at me and spoke: "I know that."

"Allen, one more time I must speak to you about Christ and your need to make things right with Him."

Allen paused and said, "I'm ready now." We bowed our heads at the side of that bed and he gave his heart to Jesus Christ. Allen looked up at me and a radiant smile illuminated his whole face. He looked up at the foot of his bed and with breathless excitement he said, "Can you see them?"

I said, "See what?"

He said, "Can you see all the angels standing around at the foot of my bed? They're singing!"

"Well, Allen, I can't see them and I can't hear them, but I know they are there. God's Word says that when you accept Christ as your Savior all the angels in heaven rejoice. Your name today is written in the Book of Life, and you will inherit eternal life."

That evening at 8:05 P.M. my phone rang. Allen had joined the angels in heaven.

***"Imagine a woman who has ten coins and loses one. Won't she light a lamp and scour the house, looking in every nook and cranny until she finds it? And when she finds it you can be sure she'll call her friends and neighbors: 'Celebrate with me! I found my lost coin!' Count on it—that's the kind of party God's angels throw every time one lost soul turns to God."***

Luke 15:8-10, MSG

TWENTY-THREE

# Did You Know My Neighbor, God?

J.P. WAS NINE when we moved into the house on Lexington Drive. Our next-door neighbors, Sandy and Tom, had three children. Fun-loving, these involved parents coached local hockey teams and had season tickets to the Michigan State University football games. Sandy's contagious laugh could be heard a block away. She loved life—and everybody knew it!

I liked Sandy from the first time I met her. Our back yards were divided by an invisible property line, and over the next ten years we had numerous opportunities to chat with each other as we watered and weeded our gardens. I often wondered what Sandy's spiritual background was, but I didn't want to be pushy. After all, we were neighbors. Once she commented about seeing one of my books in an area bookstore. I wanted to be careful about coming on too strong about God. I often thought about inviting her to an outreach event at my church, but the timing didn't seem right. Both of our families were so busy.

Sandy loved roses. She had planted a large rose garden on the side of her house and was the neighborhood's rose expert. For her birthday, Sandy's brother constructed a picturesque brick walkway beside the roses and topped it off with an arched, white arbor. It looked like a fairyland—and it faced my family room window.

Mid-August came. Sandy and I hadn't seen much of each other. I was in my back yard watering flowers when Sandy stepped outside to do the same.

"Sandy," I yelled across the yard. "Your roses are more beautiful than ever."

"Well," she said, smiling, "our son is graduating from high school next spring, and I want the yard to be pretty for his open house. It's hard to believe the time flies by so quickly."

I was thinking the same thing. Time. It *did* move swiftly. We had lived next door for ten years, and although I had a very congenial relationship with my neighbor, I had never even invited her over for coffee—*in ten years*.

She smiled and waved as she turned and walked up the steps of her porch. I thought about inviting her to the Salad Supper outreach event our women's ministries group was sponsoring, but I felt awkward about bringing up the subject.

The following day was filled with answering correspondence and daily housekeeping chores. Gene and I had a late dinner. The next morning my doorbell rang. It was another neighbor. As I opened the door, Mary stuck her head inside. She was breathless. "Have you heard about Sandy?"

"No," I said. "Is something wrong?"

Mary's words ran together. "Yesterday she went to work as usual and she had a severe headache. During the day the headache got worse, and her coworkers took her to the hospital. The pain didn't let up very much, so they decided to keep her there overnight. Tom was at the hospital with her last night and she said, 'Honey, the kids need you more than I do. You go home and I'll see you in the morning.'"

I could see tears in Mary's eyes. She went on. "At four

this morning she had an aneurysm and the scan shows flat brain waves. They'll do another scan in twenty-four hours, but the prognosis doesn't look good."

Sandy never woke up. On Wednesday morning she was pronounced dead, and that evening teams of doctors from university hospitals flew in by helicopter to harvest her organs. On Friday afternoon I attended my neighbor's memorial service.

***Be ready to speak up and tell anyone who asks why you're living the way you are, and always with the utmost courtesy. Keep a clear conscience before God.***

1 Peter 3:15-16, MSG

TWENTY-FOUR

# My Favorite Sin

FOR MOST OF US, it's "the small stuff" that depletes our spiritual energy and leaves us defeated and frustrated. The Enemy consistently suggests that our trivial self-defeating behaviors are no big deal. Yet, we feel powerless to change old habits. Here is the story of one young woman who, with God's help, found the power to change.

Heather's laugh could be identified from across a room. Her eyes twinkled with delicious mischief, and her infectious enthusiasm drew a crowd within minutes of her entering the room.

> "When temptaion knocks at the door, I ask Jesus to open the door. That is very safe."
>
> —CORRIE TEN BOOM, *Clippings from My Notebook*

I was thrilled to learn that she worked as a youth specialist and frequently spoke at retreats for teenagers. She had come to a "Speak Up with Confidence" seminar to hone her speaking skills—but she was a "natural" already. Throughout the weekend I was encouraged to realize leaders with giftedness like Heather were still venturing into youth ministry.

One week following the seminar she wrote me a letter. The honesty, vulnerability, and courage it took to pen the words she wrote stirred my heart. After her opening comments, she wrote:

> My teen years were very difficult. I chose the role of prodigal daughter to try and get my parents' attention. Running away from home, getting into trouble at school, and smoking pot daily were some of the choices I made.
>
> In my first year of marriage, I found myself picking up one of my old habits—smoking pot. Not on a regular basis . . . but the habit was back in my life.
>
> I always rationalized it was no big deal—I never smoked around the children. I would only smoke with a very few adults who could be trusted, and I hardly ever did it. All of this was true, but it still bothered me for three reasons:
>
> 1. What if my oldest daughter, now nine, should wake from sleep some night and find her mother with marijuana?
> 2. Part of my personal testimony to teens included a story of my old lifestyle. What if on a retreat a teen should ask me if I've smoked pot since then?
> 3. I was haunted by the line in Scripture that says we should live a life that is *blameless*. I knew pot was illegal.
>
> During the conference you were giving the teaching on putting together one's personal testimony. The Scripture that leaped off the page to me was: "Therefore, if anyone is in Christ, he is a new creation; *the old has gone*, the new has come!" (2 Corinthians 5:17, emphasis added).
>
> The Word of God just pierced my heart and it

became crystal clear to me: SMOKING POT HAD NO PLACE IN MY BEING A NEW CREATION IN CHRIST!

I knew what I had to do, but Satan tried to talk me out of it. He kept trying to convince me it was no big deal since I smoked pot so infrequently. Then for our Bible study you gave us the assignment of preparing a three-minute message. I chose the passage from Philippians 3. My eyes kept going back to verse 8: "Jesus Christ my Lord, for whom I have suffered the loss of all things, and count them but rubbish in order that I may gain Christ" (NASB).

I did an alliterative outline:

1. *Put* behind.

2. *Press* on for the prize.

As I involved my small group in action movements to match my outline, I proceeded with my speech. No one knew at the time, but I knew that as I spoke, I made the definite decision to put my old habit behind me!

As we ended our small group speeches, I was feeling anxious about my new decision and decided to ask my group if they would stay afterwards to pray with me. I felt so blessed to have found prayer support with newfound sisters in Christ at a time when I needed it. I shared my burden; they prayed, and I cried tears of gratefulness to God.

I had ended my speech earlier that day with these words: "Think about the prize. It's worth it! *He* is worth it. So as for me, *I will press on in running the race, forgetting what lies behind, straining forward to what lies ahead*.

Heather ended her letter with these words: "I am so relieved. This has always been a stumbling block for me. I have told an accountability partner my commitment, so I won't turn back. . . ."

*You've all been to the stadium and seen the athletes race. Everyone runs; one wins. Run to win. All good athletes train hard. They do it for a gold medal that tarnishes and fades. You're after one that's gold eternally.*

*I don't know about you, but I'm running hard for the finish line. I'm giving it everything I've got. No sloppy living for me! I'm staying alert and in top condition. I'm not going to get caught napping, telling everyone else all about it and then missing out myself.*

1 Corinthians 9:24-27, MSG

TWENTY-FIVE

# Do We Have to Move—Again?

GENE AND I HAD just returned from a Florida convention when we received word that a good friend and business colleague of Gene's had been jogging in his subdivision and suddenly keeled over and died. An autopsy revealed that he had an aneurysm. Jerry was only forty-nine years old. We were heartsick for his family and deeply mourned the loss of our friend.

A few weeks later I was at home when the phone rang. I picked up the receiver; it was Gene. "Carol, I have important news. Are you sitting down?"

I didn't know what to expect. He continued, "When Jerry passed away, he left a large clientele in Port Huron, Michigan. I have been asked to take over the position as soon as possible. His clients need service. I know it's hard enough for us to realize Jerry is no longer alive, but someone needs to keep his office open. It's really a wonderful business opportunity. Many of his clients used to go to your dad's church. It feels like a good fit for my skills, too. What do you think?"

I was already skilled in providing a response to the "Do you want to move?" question. I had my speech rehearsed.

"Honey, it's so wonderful that we know you are the company's *first choice* for this position, even though we are so happy here that we'd never move. Right?" I was once again trying to tactfully play the role of the Holy Spirit in Gene's life.

He wasn't deterred. He continued, "We really need to pray about this. It would be a great move for our future. Michigan is our home state, so we could see our families more often. J.P. could spend time with his grandparents on a regular basis. And Port Huron is right on the water. We *love* water! That's where the Saint Clair River opens up into Lake Huron. I think we should think seriously about accepting this business offer. An opportunity like this might never come around again."

My heart hurt. I was in my *dream* job! Our last move had occurred when Gene accepted a position in the home office of the insurance company in Fort Wayne, where he worked in business insurance. After moving to Indiana, I taught English in the local Christian school and we had begun attending a dynamic, growing local church. Within a few months I was asked to become the director of women's ministries. When the school year ended, I gave my full attention to the church staff position.

I began writing Bible study materials and teaching a weekly class for women. On the first day of the Bible study 225 women attended. Many of them accepted Christ, and others were growing in their faith. I loved this ministry and I loved these women. How could my husband ask me to move—*again?*

After much prayer, we put our house up for sale and made the move to Port Huron, Michigan. In my heart I was rebellious, unhappy, and depressed. My husband had a challenging, fulfilling, exciting career—but within a year and a half I had left the two most rewarding jobs I had ever experienced. It was *unfair!*

One month after the move Gene was out of town on business. The women in my Bible study in Fort Wayne were having their end-of-the-Bible-study-year luncheon. I wasn't there and I wanted to celebrate my misery with a pity party. Since I didn't have any friends in this new city yet, I decided to take my then four-year-old son out for lunch. Sitting in a window booth in a local restaurant, I encouraged J.P. to draw pictures on his place mat once we were finished with our meal.

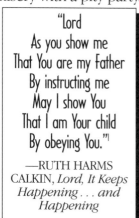

> "Lord
> As you show me
> That You are my Father
> By instructing me
> May I show You
> That I am Your child
> By obeying You."[1]
>
> —RUTH HARMS CALKIN, *Lord, It Keeps Happening . . . and Happening*

I casually glanced out the window and saw cars passing by. I wasn't prepared for what happened next. I began to see women in many of those cars, and God spoke to me through the inner impression of the heart. He said, "Carol, the women in this city are just as needy as the women you left in Fort Wayne, Indiana. When will you quit bucking against what I have done in your life and commit yourself to My purpose in bringing you to this city? I have a plan for *you* here, as well as for Gene."

I simply said, "Yes, Lord." With those two simple words I was submitting to His authority in my life and committing to actively looking for His purpose in bringing me to this place. I was tired of the loneliness and sick of the depression. Matthew 5:3-4 (MSG) described my feelings. *You're blessed when you're at the end of your rope. . . . You're blessed when you feel you've lost what is most dear to you. Only then can you be embraced by the One most dear to you.*

J.P. and I went home, and I put him in bed for his afternoon nap. An hour later the phone rang. It was a woman I had never met before. She said, "My name is Sherrie Eldridge and I'm an American living in Canada. My husband was transferred here with the Dow Chemical Company a few years ago." Sherrie had come to know the Lord in a Bible study in California before making this move.

She continued, "Carol, I've been meeting with a group of about thirty neighbors for the last two years, and we've been praying for a Bible study teacher. Somebody told me you like to teach the Bible. Is there any chance that you would teach us?"

I was stunned. What happened over the next few months still seems like a miracle to me. Port Huron is one of the main border crossing points between Ontario, Canada, and Michigan. Our two countries are connected by the Blue Water Bridge. Sherrie and I began the first international Bible Study Fellowship program, with women attending from both the United States and Canada. Within a short time there were 350 women enrolled in the Wednesday morning Bible class—and 40 percent of them were coming through customs to attend!

At the border crossing, you always have to answer the questions of the customs officer. Usually they are quite predictable: "What is your citizenship? What is your purpose for entering the country? How long will you be staying? Are you carrying any firearms? Do you have any goods to declare?" Every week the Canadian women would respond to these questions before coming to the Bible study.

On one Wednesday morning the customs official asked one of the women, "What is your purpose for entering the country?"

"Bible study," she responded.

The man hit his forehead with the flat of his hand as he groaned, "Oh, no! Is that Bible study on again today?"

On another occasion one of the customs officers asked, "What is your purpose for entering the country?"

The Canadian woman answered, "Bible study."

The officer put both hands in the air and said, "Oh, good! I'm a brand-new Christian and I have this deep theological question I wanted to ask one of you—but I couldn't remember which day you come through."

The woman quickly interjected, "Oh, don't ask me. I'm a brand-new Christian too! But do you see that woman in the car behind mine? She knows her Bible really well—and I'm sure she can help you out!"

As I continued teaching the Bible class, God began to work in my heart—as well as in the lives of the members of the weekly study. The women in this city *were* just as needy as the women I left in Fort Wayne, Indiana. And now God had opened doors to Canada, too! God *did* have an important reason for bringing me to this place. But I had been so upset with my husband for dragging me from my former position of security and significance that I couldn't see His purpose.

One day I opened my devotional book and read, "All that I have seen teaches me to trust the Creator for all that I have not seen." It was a lesson for a lifetime.

***Trust God from the bottom of your heart;***
***don't try to figure out everything on your own.***
***Listen for God's voice in everything you do,***
***everywhere you go;***
***he's the one who will keep you on track.***

Proverbs 3:5-6, MSG

*I had been in California for five days of training to become a Bible Study Fellowship teaching leader. It was the longest time I had ever been away from my child. I missed my family and could hardly wait to see my husband and son again.*

*As I jumped out of the car, my four-year-old son, J.P., gave me an enormous grin and sprang into action. As I caught him up in my arms, we twirled around in a couple of circles to celebrate our reunion. My exuberant child squeezed me tightly as he shouted, "Oh, Mommy, Mommy! When I saw you right now, it was just like I saw you brand-new!"*

*Sometimes applications are instant. My son's precious words reminded me of how God sees me through His Son's shed blood on Calvary. If I have confessed my sin and accepted His forgiveness, I am a new person. Instead of seeing my*

*transgressions and mistakes of the past,*
*He sees me clothed in Jesus' righteousness.*
*He sees me as brand-new and beautiful!*

PART SIX

# When You Want Others to Know God

TWENTY-SIX

# The Funeral, the Alcoholic, and the Preacher

IT WAS THE FIRST DAY of kindergarten, and Cindy was excited about wearing the brand-new shoes her mom had bought her for the big day. As she was crossing the street that morning, she was looking down at her beautiful shoes—and she never saw the car that hit her.

My father, Clyde Afman, who had recently accepted the invitation to become the pastor of this, his first church, spoke at Cindy's funeral. Cindy had natural curly hair that hung in blond ringlets around her face. In that stark, white coffin she looked like a porcelain doll. Too young. Too beautiful. Too soon.

Dad first met Ace at that funeral. Cindy was his niece, the daughter of Ace's brother. Ace loved her deeply and was very upset by this horrible accident. He had been drinking before coming to the funeral. People had told him the new preacher in town was making the rounds and had been calling on folks in the area. When he met Dad, Ace looked up, and with a slurred voice he muttered, "Well, Preacher, when are you gonna come and visit me?" Dad made the appointment, and Mom and Dad later made the visit.

I'll never forget Dad's first description of Ace: "He was

a drunk, a wife-beater, and wouldn't even have had a house to live in apart from the grace of his father-in-law." Ace drank up his money, and his father-in-law often bought the groceries for his daughter, Sheri, and their three children.

Some time later Dad visited Ace in the hospital where he was drying out from booze. He wasn't buying into the gospel yet, but the Spirit of God was at work in his heart.

Ace and Sheri had an old television set that could only get three channels. That week the only program that came in was "The Billy Graham Crusade." Ace was irritated, but he had nothing else to watch, so for three consecutive nights he listened—and God used Billy Graham to prepare the way for a visit from Mom and Dad the next evening. That night after they heard the gospel once again, Ace and Sheri invited Jesus Christ to be their personal Savior.

As Ace walked Mom and Dad to the front door, he said, "How much do I owe you, Preacher?" He figured something so wonderful must come with a price tag.

Dad smiled and responded, "You don't owe me anything, Ace. It's free."

Ace and Sheri began attending church faithfully. Within a short time they were baptized. Ace had heard about tithing and that you're supposed to give part of your money to God, so he immediately began giving liberally to the work of the Lord.

However, the Enemy was relentless. Ace's mother was a spiritualist medium, and there had been a lot of satanic activity in their home. At times Ace's desire for alcohol would be so intense as he drove home from work that he would yell at the top of his lungs, "Lord, the Devil's after me again! Help me!" And He did.

Despite the Enemy's temptations, Ace's life took a 180-degree turn. He began treating Sheri with dignity and respect. With her help, he memorized John 3:16 and began carrying his Bible to work, even though he was illiterate.

Ace began learning how to read so he could understand the Word of God, and he'd often sit during his lunch break with an open Bible in his lap. Many of his old cronies at the Buick Motor Company in Flint, Michigan, were bikers and drinking buddies. He desired to witness to them, but he was scared. He prayed, "God if You want me to talk to these guys about You, You'll have to send them over here."

Before long, one came. And then another. And another. They had realized that what their buddy had experienced was *real*. Ace didn't have to stand on a soapbox and preach. He became God's instrument to lead *many* of them to Christ. With the help of his wife and daughter, Ace studied the Scriptures, and during his lunch breaks he led Bible studies for these new believers at the factory.

> "Jesus Christ didn't commit the gospel to an advertising agency; He commissioned disciples. And He didn't command them to pass out tracts; He said that they would be His witnesses."
>
> —JOE BAYLY, *The Gospel Blimp*

Ace never lost his zeal for God.

My dad, now ministering in another church, recently heard a speaker who is a missionary serving in Brazil. As Gordon recounted his testimony, Dad's heart was moved. Gordon had blatantly rejected God and was adamantly opposed to the gospel. But his sister and her husband lived in Flint, Michigan, and his brother-in-law worked at Buick Motor Company.

Gordon told of how a coworker had witnessed to his brother-in-law and led him to Christ. In turn, his brother-in-law's wife responded to the gospel. They began to pray for Gordon. After four years, God answered their prayers. Gordon and his wife surrendered their lives to Christ, accepted the call to missions, and now serve God in Brazil.

And the coworker's name? You've already guessed, haven't you? Ace Spencer.

And the story continues. . . .

*One man died for everyone. That puts everyone in the same boat. He included everyone in his death so that everyone could also be included in his life, a resurrection life, a far better life than people ever lived on their own.*

*Because of this decision we don't evaluate people by what they have or how they look. . . . Anyone united with the Messiah gets a fresh start, is created new. The old life is gone; a new life burgeons! Look at it! All this comes from the God who settled the relationship between us and him. . . . God put the world square with himself through the Messiah, giving the world a fresh start by offering forgiveness of sins. God has given us the task of telling everyone what he is doing. We're Christ's representatives.*

2 Corinthians 5:14-20, MSG

TWENTY-SEVEN

# The Death Threat

THE FOLLOWING NARRATIVE was given to me by Mary G. Block, a missionary in Bogota, Colombia. Life in Bogota can be extremely dangerous and difficult, as this account shows. It is the story of Obed Montanez Guerrero and is his tribute to the faithfulness of God.

It was Sunday, April 14, 1991. I had to work my shift as a customs officer at the Bogota International Airport. I got up at 4:00 A.M. and had my daily prayer time. I showered and while I was shaving in front of the mirror, I suddenly saw myself in a coffin inside an amphitheater. I felt overwhelmed and rebuked the spirit of death in the name of the Lord Jesus Christ. Instantly, all fear left me, and I continued to get ready.

At 4:45 A.M. I left for work in my red Renault 9 car, using the same route I always take. Suddenly, from out of nowhere, a car came upon me. The car was going the wrong way on a one-way street, headed directly toward the front of my car. I thought the driver was drunk and pulled my car to the side of the road to avoid an accident.

When I reached the corner, four men got out of the car, all armed with guns. They began to hit the car windows and threatened to kill me if I did not open them immediately. I opened the car door in order to give them the vehicle and avoid more trouble, but they shoved me violently back into the car.

They took my documents, money, clothes, and shoes, dividing all of my belongings between them like birds of prey. Then they beat me unmercifully and treated me in an obscene manner. Then they tried to kill me by making me drink a liquid that had poison in it. However, the first bottle had no effect on me, so they made me drink a second bottle.

In those moments I remembered the words of our Lord from Mark 16:18 (KJV), "If they drink any deadly thing, it shall not hurt them." At the same time I remembered a promise that my mother had given me when I left home for the first time:

> Even though I walk
>     through the valley of the shadow of death,
> I will fear no evil,
>     for you are with me;
> your rod and your staff,
>     they comfort me. (Psalm 23:4)

All the while I was in the hands of the thieves, they talked about killing me and leaving me where no one would find me. But the whole time I felt the angels of the Lord surrounding me and protecting me. I did not feel any pain during the time of the beating and the cutting on my back.

After torturing me, the men talked about shooting me. Then they decided I was so beat up I would die shortly anyway, so they threw me into a garbage bin.

I waited fifteen or twenty minutes after they left and then

crawled out of the bin. It was a cold morning. Dressed only in my underwear, I ran for about half an hour to the nearest police station. Later, I was picked up by family members.

At the time of the attack, my wife was in another city attending a committee meeting for leaders in our denomination. As soon as she got word of my situation, she came immediately and, together, we gave thanks to the Lord Jesus for sparing my life.

> "The refiner is never very far from the mouth of the furnace when his gold is in the fire."
>
> —CHARLES SPURGEON, *A Rainbow of Hope*

As we struggled to make sense of the situation I had just been through, many questions troubled us: Why did we lose the car that we were going to sell in order to take care of a current serious economic need? Why did this happen to us when we were people who were committed to the ministry of the Lord?

The police told us that stolen cars are usually taken apart immediately and the parts are sold, so there was very little chance we would ever get our vehicle back. Daily, we put our petition regarding the car before the Lord at our family altar.

After several months my faith began to weaken, but our little five-year-old daughter continued to pray with fervor and conviction. That encouraged us to keep trusting the Lord. But then, without warning, I lost my job as a customs officer. I had worked at the airport for years, and there was no explanation for why my position was terminated.

Then unexpectedly, my wife received a phone call from someone who said he knew where our car was and that it was in good condition. He asked to have an appointment with us and for us to sign a power of attorney for him to rescue the car.

We were troubled. It seemed that this could be a trap, and we asked the church to pray with us for wisdom. That night our missionary friend, Mary Block, prayed with us. After considering all the circumstances, we felt the Lord was leading us to go ahead with confidence and meet with the man.

We did just that. Before we left for the appointment, we prayed and asked the Lord to go with us. We met the man and signed the paper giving him the power of attorney. Then, miraculously, after *sixteen months* of being without our car, it was returned to us *in perfect condition!* God had answered our prayers!

We held a thanksgiving service in our home and invited our church family and friends. It was a celebration of praise to our almighty God for saving my life and for returning our car.

I remembered the words of the doctor as he examined my open wounds following the beating: "How could you have suffered so much torture?" At the time of this severe beating I felt no pain even though the healing process was agonizing. Along with my doctor and my family, I realized this supernatural strength during the attack had come from God.

Now, instead of working as a customs officer, my wife and I are pastoring a church in Medellin, Colombia. We praise God for His protection over our lives.

*God, my shepherd!*
*I don't need a thing.*
*You have bedded me down in lush meadows,*
*you find me quiet pools to drink from.*
*True to your word,*
*you let me catch my breath*
*and send me in the right direction.*

*Even when the way goes through*
*Death Valley,*
*I'm not afraid*
*when you walk at my side.*

*Your trusty shepherd's crook*
*makes me feel secure.*

*You serve me a six-course dinner*
*right in front of my enemies.*
*You revive my drooping head;*
*my cup brims with blessing.*

*Your beauty and love chase after me*
*every day of my life.*
*I'm back home in the house of God*
*for the rest of my life.*

Psalm 23, MSG

TWENTY-EIGHT

# The Unexpected Confession

I WAS AUTOGRAPHING books at the close of a conference when I noticed a long line of retreat participants waiting to say goodbye. The woman who was next in line had a request. "Would you please autograph this book for my friend? She couldn't be here this weekend."

I immediately responded, "I'd be glad to." Since I knew the book was being purchased for someone else, I instinctively asked, "Is she a believer?" I wanted to write an appropriate comment in the front of the book.

She hesitated, then said, "Well, *she* is, but I'm not."

Now the woman had my full attention. She had just sat through four talks I had given over a three-day retreat weekend. I had given several opportunities for women to respond to the gospel. Quickly glancing at her name tag, I looked her in the eyes and said, "Chris, how did you happen to come to this conference?"

She paused and smiled. "Well, I have this religious friend, and I actually came to get her off my back, if you know what I mean." I could feel her evaluating the situation and my response, wondering if it was a safe place to make such a shocking statement. I tried not to look too surprised.

She continued, "I guess you could describe me as the intellectual type. I've been studying the great religions of the world. I've been evaluating Buddhism. Those Muslims interest me a lot, too. They cling so tenaciously to their beliefs. I've also visited a number of churches in the Toronto area, and Christianity is just one more of the religions I'm investigating."

As she paused, I entered the conversation again. "Well, Chris, you heard a whole lot about Christianity this weekend. What do you think?"

> "When you say a situation or a person is hopeless, you are slamming the door in the face of God."
>
> —CHARLES L. ALLEN, *A Rainbow of Hope*

Chris was confident, direct, and sincere. "I hope this doesn't offend you, but I'm really puzzled. I've listened to you talk for three days, and I think you are a very intelligent woman. It really surprises me that you actually believe in the inerrancy of the Bible."

By this time many of the women who were still waiting in line were praying for Chris. I spoke thoughtfully. "Chris, you are an educated, thinking woman who is in a serious pursuit of truth. Have you ever *read* the Bible?"

"Not really," she responded.

I tactfully confronted her. "I would think someone as intelligent as you are wouldn't even think of rejecting Christianity until you've at least read through the Bible once. If you're willing to accept the challenge, I want to encourage you to start reading in the gospel of John."

With a straightforward look, she responded, "I guess I could do that." She thanked me for my time and said goodbye.

Two days later an overnight letter arrived at the conference center. It was addressed to me. I opened it and read:

Dear Carol,

Thank you for talking to me at the conference. I appreciated your presentations. Thanks for taking the time to autograph the book for my friend. I'm sure she'll enjoy it. I've been thinking a lot about Christianity and I *will* read the Bible. At this time *I remain skeptical, but envious*, and I shall remember this experience. . . .

Sincerely,
Chris

***The unspiritual self, just as it is by nature,***
***can't receive the gifts of God's Spirit.***
***There's no capacity for them.***
***They seem like so much silliness.***
***Spirit can be known only by spirit—***
***God's Spirit and our spirits in open communion.***
***Spiritually alive, we have access to everything***
***God's Spirit is doing.***

1 Corinthians 2:14-15, MSG

TWENTY-NINE

# Daisy's Best Advice

DAISY ENTERTAINED with ease. She loved people and people loved her back. Her home was filled with memories of precious events and people. Daisy's family had immigrated to Canada from Northern Ireland, and every part of the house contained nostalgic reminders of a respected heritage: a teapot with matching china cups, figurines, books with personalized inscriptions, handmade lace doilies under stately old lamps, pictures of family members and friends in antique gold frames.

> "I have held many things in my hands, and I have lost them all; but whatever I have placed in God's hands, that I still possess."
>
> —CORRIE TEN BOOM, *Clippings from My Notebook*

Some people "have folks in" because they have space available and "somebody needs to do it." Others invite overnight company because one of their greatest joys is to provide a home away from home for family, friends, or people in ministry who are passing through. As I entered Daisy's home, I felt wanted, welcomed, and significant. She served me piping hot tea, complete with fruit and cheese on precious flowered china plates—and there beside my fork was a freshly ironed linen napkin. I felt like royalty.

When Daisy spoke, I felt her passion for God. She was very involved in her local church and was a leader in a Christian women's organization. In fact, she had invited me to come and train local women in how to share their personal testimonies with a clear explanation of the gospel. Evangelism was an important part of her ministry.

During my stay, she described her heart for missions. She and her husband had gone to Central America on several short-term trips with an optometric group. Throughout the year they collected used eyeglasses from individuals who needed to update their prescription lenses. They took those glasses to the mission field where they could be recycled in third world countries.

I tried to imagine this refined lady at a remote mission station—with no china cups, ironed linens, indoor plumbing, or sanitized kitchen. Somehow the concept of "rats, roaches, and rice" didn't fit the profile of the woman before me, but she was willing to sacrifice her personal comfort for her passion to serve God and reveal Him to others.

In one of our many conversations during that three-day period, Daisy made a statement that has stayed with me to this day: *"Attitudes are the quiet judgments that shape our lives; they mold the form that living takes."* I don't know if it was original with her or if she was quoting from someone else, but it made an impact on my life.

A couple of years later I heard from a mutual friend that Daisy's home had been broken into during one of their mission trips. Most of her prized possessions and cherished antiques brought from her native Northern Ireland had been stolen. I knew the treasured memories that were represented by those objects—and I felt devastated for her.

Some time later, I saw Daisy again. With a peaceful smile,

she responded to my questions about her loss. "They were only *things*," she said, "only *things*."

Daisy's words that day reminded me of something Corrie ten Boom said, "You must always learn to hold things loosely, because if you don't, it will hurt too deeply when they are taken away from you."[1]

***"Don't hoard treasure down here where it gets eaten by moths and corroded by rust or—worse!—stolen by burglars. Stockpile treasure in heaven, where it's safe from moth and rust and burglars. It's obvious, isn't it? The place where your treasure is, is the place you will most want to be, and end up being."***

Matthew 6:19-21, MSG

THIRTY

# The Unwanted Seat

MY SISTER BONNIE and I were leaving picturesque Vancouver, British Columbia. We had just completed a "Speak Up with Confidence" communications training seminar for about one hundred emerging Christian leaders. Rarely had we worked with such highly motivated participants—and we were exhausted.

We had opted to spend Saturday night in an airport hotel to save on airfare. We also wanted to use a couple of Delta Airlines tickets before they expired, which required us to fly from Vancouver to Los Angeles, then on to Dayton, with a final leg to Detroit. (This was *not* a direct route home.)

My neighbor is my travel agent, and he always books an aisle seat for me. And when Bonnie accompanies me for speaker training seminars, he reserves us aisle seats across from each other, so we can stretch our legs, have access to the aisle without climbing over passengers, and talk to each other with ease.

When we took our seats for the flight to Los Angeles, I found myself next to the most talkative, flirtatious, dominant, and aggressive man I had met in a long time. He obviously had alcohol for breakfast and wanted to give me advice on investments (his specialty), vacation spots, and travel tips. I politely thanked him for his advice, then closed my eyes, hoping to indicate that the conversation was finished. But he was not discouraged. The man never quit talking from liftoff to touchdown.

During the layover Bonnie and I ordered a couple of cappuccinos at a specialty coffee shop, and she offered me some unwanted but timely advice. "Carol, we have worked hard all weekend. We have taught seminar participants, answered questions, facilitated small groups, endured a three-hour time change—and we are exhausted. You sat next to the most talkative man we have ever met on the last flight, and you allowed him to engage you in an ongoing response to his questions. Do not, I repeat, *do not* speak to the person sitting next to you on this flight. In fact, don't even *look* at the person, so you won't be tempted to talk. We deserve some rest. Close your eyes and sleep."

We boarded the flight to Dayton, and to my surprise and irritation my travel agent had made a major mistake in booking our seat assignments. Bonnie had the coveted aisle seat, a businessman was sandwiched in the middle seat, and I had the window seat and would be pinned in for a four-hour flight on an overbooked, very crowded flight. I was *not* a happy camper.

As I climbed over the feet of the businessman, I said, "Excuse me, sir." He was reading a Tom Clancy novel. "Are you enjoying the book?" I queried. Bonnie was shooting visual daggers in my direction.

The man responded, "Yes, it's a great plot. Have you read the book?"

"No, but my husband and son have both read it, and they really enjoy Clancy's writing style."

Bonnie's body language and glaring eye contact were warning me that I was entering into a conversation that might last for hours. But I ignored her and the dialogue continued.

The man identified himself as Brad and told me he had a brand-new job with a hamburger chain. He was en route to Detroit to scout out some new business locations for the company. The job was a financial "dream come true," but he said his wife had recently left him. He had two children and feared not seeing them as often as a dad should. There was a deep sadness in the man's spirit, and I sensed a profound spiritual need.

Brad went on. "The divorce was my fault. I hung out with the guys and made sporting events my whole life. My wife had every right to leave me—and now I think it's too late to get her back."

By this time, Bonnie and I were both drawn into this man's sad story. Sensing the depth of his urgent need for God, we began to share our own spiritual journeys with him.

As the conversation continued, Brad told us his drug-addicted brother had recently moved in with him because he had nowhere else to go. "To help my brother out, I attended an Al-Anon meeting last night. I figure I need to understand more about my brother's problem in order to offer assistance. You two remind me a lot of some of the people I met there."

As I shared a brief overview of my own discovery of the gospel and who Jesus is, I realized that a fortyish businessman could read mixed motives in a woman seated next to him on a plane explaining the gospel to him. I instinctively said, "Brad, you seem to have some deep spiritual needs and an interest in finding the answers to life's most searching questions."

I discovered he was from the greater Los Angeles area and immediately said, "I have some friends who attend a great church in your area. Their pastor is a guy named

Chuck Swindoll, and I think you would really relate to him. Would you mind if I gave them your name and phone number, so they could get in touch with you?"

With sincerity, Brad responded, "I'd really appreciate that."

Bonnie and I continued to talk about our families and of God's work in our lives. After a pause, Brad smiled and looked at us as he said, "Okay, I give up. *Just exactly how do I get what you two have?*"

Now I was in shock! This man was *begging* us to lead him to Christ.

I said, "Brad, it's very simple, but sometimes people try to make it complicated. The Bible teaches that God sent His Son, Jesus, to this earth. He was sinless and perfect. He grew to maturity and went into His public teaching ministry at the age of thirty. The religious leaders of the day didn't recognize Him as the Savior of the world. They mocked Him and ridiculed Him. At age thirty-three He went through the most painful death invented by mankind—death by crucifixion. It was a death that was so horrible it was saved for foreigners and slaves. Jesus hung on a cross and paid the price for all of the wrongdoing in the world—my sin, and yours. But the story doesn't end there. He rose again and He's in heaven today preparing a place for those who believe."

> "The gospel message is designed by God to touch men and women at the core of their beings. The gospel specializes in awakening lost sinners to the vacuum in their hearts that can be filled only by Jesus Christ."
>
> —MARK McCLOSKEY, *Tell It Often, Tell It Well*

I concluded, "Brad, I don't think it was an accident that you got the undesirable center seat between two sisters on this crowded plane. God knew you needed to find Him in the middle of all that's happening in your life right now. Are you interested in following me in a prayer to invite Christ into your life right now?"

"Oh yes," he responded. The three of us bowed our heads as Brad vocalized his desire to invite Jesus Christ to be his Savior and Lord. He prayed right out loud with no embarrassment and no hesitation. I found myself wiping tears, ashamed of my attitude when I discovered my assigned seat was in such an unwanted place. Even though Bonnie and I both thought I needed to rest, God saw the big picture.

When I got home, I realized I wasn't that tired. The joy of praying with this man had restored my soul.

Perhaps God knew that Brad would never again be as open to the gospel as he was at that time. I don't know, but I do know that God wants people to know Him, and He provides all kinds of opportunities. I believe He planned this important meeting for a businessman and two tired sisters. Bonnie and I were once again amazed at how God works and provides—and Brad's life was changed forever.

***God didn't go to all the trouble of sending his Son merely to point an accusing finger, telling the world how bad it was. He came to help, to put the world right again. Anyone who trusts in him is acquitted.***

John 3:17-18, MSG

THIRTY-ONE

# The Face I Can't Forget

EASTER WEEKEND was fast approaching. Gene and I had made plans to pick up J.P. at the U.S. Naval Academy, and then we were going to spend a family weekend together in our nation's capital. Upon arriving in Annapolis, we parked on the stately grounds of the grand old military institution and eagerly walked to Bancroft Hall to let J.P. know we had arrived. He rushed downstairs in uniform, and we left for Washington, D.C.

J.P. quickly caught us up on his recent academic and military challenges. I marveled at how grown-up and mature he was as he enthusiastically discussed history and politics with his father. For a few minutes I indulged in a mixed feeling of sadness for the child I was letting go of—and a deep sense of pride in the adult who was emerging.

"What shall we do in Washington?" he asked with anticipation. "My buddies and I *love* that city, and I know you would enjoy going through the Smithsonian, and the Capitol building, and we *have* to see the Vietnam Veterans Memorial. And why don't we try to get into the Holocaust museum? I haven't been there yet and I hear it's an awesome place. What do you think?"

We were eager to have J.P. take us on a tour of all that had become so meaningful to him during his first two years of academy life. We toured the Capitol building and looked up our congressman's office. He wasn't in, but we took a picture in front of his nameplate.

Later, we drove to the Vietnam memorial. As we approached the huge black wall bearing the names of the thousands of young men and women who gave their lives in the service of our country, silence enveloped us. People were touching names on the wall, weeping quietly for a lost loved one. Flowers were pressed into the cracks between sections of the wall at various intervals. A few people were doing charcoal "rubbings" with parchment placed over the name of their lost relative.

Gene and I checked the directory and found the name of one of our classmates who had died in the war—LaMotte Horsely, class of '65, Durand Area High School. There it was, etched in black marble. I wondered if LaMotte knew Jesus. As I pressed my finger against the indentation of his name printed in stone, tears flowed uncontrollably. It was a poignant reminder of how fortunate I was to have my husband—alive.

The next day we toured the Holocaust Memorial Museum. As we entered the building, a hush fell over the once animated crowd. The visitor's guide, a brochure, describes the graphic reason for the construction of this memorial:

> The United States Holocaust Memorial Museum is dedicated to presenting the history of the persecution and murder of six million Jews and millions of other victims of Nazi tyranny from 1933 to 1945.

I cringed. These atrocities were taking place during my parents' lifetime, and up until two years before I was born!

It was easier to imagine this evil being done by barbarians early in the history of civilization. Not so.

The brochure explained further:

> The Museum's primary mission is to inform Americans about this unprecedented tragedy, to remember those who suffered, and to inspire visitors to contemplate the moral implications of their choices and responsibilities as citizens in an interdependent world.

We began our tour by walking through "Daniel's Story: Remember the Children," and saw the story of the Holocaust through the eyes of a child, robbed of his home, his family, and eventually, his life. It was sobering.

We took the elevator to the top floor to continue the tour. On the fourth floor, the history of the Nazi assault was graphically portrayed—man's inhumanity to man. We saw the piles of shoes that had actually been left outside the gas chambers as the Jews were told to take showers. Films documenting the medical experiments and the abuses in the work camps were shown behind half-walls that protected young children from viewing the atrocities.

> "I will not permit any man to narrow and degrade my soul by making me hate him."
>
> —BOOKER T. WASHINGTON, *Great Quotes and Illustrations*

It took several hours to complete the tour, and as we neared the end, we sat in a small amphitheater listening to the recorded oral testimonies of the survivors of the Holocaust. In spite of all the graphic footage I had seen that day, this portion of the tour turned my heart inside out.

Some of the survivors praised God for keeping them alive and for an aftermath that offered hope. But the testimony of one woman gripped my soul. She spoke of the heinous crimes that had been done to her and to her family members. As the camera closed in on her face, she trembled with anger and her voice shook as she looked with hollow eyes and spoke with conviction: *"I cannot forget, and I will not forgive!"* Her face was unforgettable.

On the drive back to Annapolis, all of us were silent. I couldn't help but think about all that I had to be grateful for. My husband didn't have to go to Vietnam. Our son was doing well in the U.S. Naval Academy. We were healthy. And we knew God's forgiveness. My nest was empty, but my heart was full.

The face of the woman at the museum still haunts me: *"I cannot forget, and I will not forgive!"* Each day we choose our own attitude. Will it be thankfulness or unforgiveness? Will we look forward or backward? Will we hurl blame or assume responsibility? Will we live with yesterday's regrets or tomorrow's opportunities?

***These are the things I go over and over,***
***emptying out the pockets of my life. . . .***

***Sometimes I ask God, my rock-solid God,***
***"Why did you let me down?***
***Why am I walking around in tears,***
***harassed by enemies?"***

Psalm 42:4,9, MSG

*Several years ago I was speaking at a seminar for Campus Crusade for Christ staff members. Everyone in the group worked in ministry on a university campus in the Midwest. One of them had found three postcards in a book in the library at Northern Michigan University. Each card was from the same individual, but they were addressed to three distinctly different people in her life.*

*To Her Parents:*

Dear Mom and Dad,

Thanks for sending me on vacation. We've toured a lot of interesting places. The historical society was really fascinating and I learned quite a bit about Marquette, Michigan, in its mining days. We've even tried some of the local food since we've been here.

Love,

Connie

*To Her Best Friend:*

Dear Sue,

Hi! I finally woke up and felt awake after one week of totally intense partying! I figured it was a good time to write before we start again. The guys up here are sensational! I went out with a different one each night. Well, take care, and don't party too much!

See ya,
Connie

*To Her Boyfriend:*

Dear Jim,

Boy, I sure do miss you! I wish you could be here so we could share the fall scenery together. I haven't been doing too much here, just visiting and touring around quite a bit. I can't wait to see you!

Love and Kisses,
Connie

PART SEVEN

# When You Learn Life Lessons from Your Kids

THIRTY-TWO

# Mom's Medal

I LIKED DONNA JON immediately. Her sense of humor was so contagious that anyone within six feet of her was caught up in the fun of whatever was happening at that moment.

A single mom, Donna Jon works in the book department at Stonecroft headquarters in Kansas City, Missouri, the parent organization for Christian Women's Clubs. Stonecroft has featured my books and Donna Jon is familiar with them, so she knew about the anxiety I had to deal with when my son pursued an appointment to the U.S. Naval Academy. (J.P.'s choice of a military career and all of the moral and ethical choices he will have to face as a naval officer is *not* the life I would have selected for my only child.)

Donna Jon and I connected as she told me of her own fears when her son, Barrett, joined the U.S. Air Force and was sent to boot camp in San Antonio, Texas. He was the squad leader for the barracks and often told his mom, "These guys don't know how to make a bed, polish their boots or their brass, or do much of any routine household task. Almost everybody in my squad owes me a pizza for helping them pass inspection!"

Barrett only met one other Christian during the six

weeks he was in boot camp. The Saturday night before graduation he called to let his mom know his flight was going to have their first leave.

That night Donna Jon called to tell her mother the news. Her mom put words to Donna Jon's fears. "Well, honey, you know what those young servicemen are like. They've been cooped up for several weeks and now they have an off-base pass. They will be going to town to drink and they'll be looking for women. You know they will be 'whooping it up' and they'll want Barrett to go with them and they'll try to get him to drink!"

> "Making the decision to have a child—it's momentous. It is to decide forever to have your heart go walking around outside your body."
>
> —ELIZABETH STONE, *A Rainbow of Hope*

Donna tried to calm her mom while subduing her own anxious heart. "Mom, you know that Barrett is grounded in the Word of God. Don't worry, we know he would *never* get into that kind of trouble." After saying goodbye, she sighed, "Oh, dear!" and prayed for her young son.

On the first night of his leave from boot camp the phone rang. When Donna Jon answered, Barrett's voice boomed on the other end of the line: "Hi, Mom!" he said cheerfully. "Well, we're finally having our first leave!" Her heart fluttered as she heard loud laughter and commotion in the background.

He went on, "Most of the guys went into town, but my friend and I decided to stay in the barracks to polish our brass. We're trying hard to make 'honor graduate'!"

Donna Jon's heart returned to a normal rate of speed, as she was reminded of all the prayers she'd sent up for her boy. God was answering . . . and He continued to answer.

Three years after entering the Air Force, Sergeant William Barrett Goddard sent his mother the following letter:

Dear Mom,

Before you read on, open the package. This is something I want you to have. It's my first medal and I would really like you to have it. It's called the Air Force Good Conduct Medal. It was granted to me for three years of perfect service to the Air Force. When I say "perfect," I mean three years without a blemish on my record. In other words, I conducted myself in the proper Air Force manner for three consecutive years.

I want you to have this for a couple of reasons. First, you've supported me more than anyone . . . in my Air Force career. You've always accepted what I had to do and I felt it was most appropriate to tell you what my plans were first.

The second reason is simple. You raised me in such a manner that I didn't have to do anything to earn this medal other than to be myself. . . . You earned this medal as much as I did. So please accept it.

Love,
Barrett

❧

At today's writing Barrett is a coach. He is a husband to Sylvia and a father of three. His oldest son, Nathan, just graduated from kindergarten *with honors*. Grandma Donna Jon tells me Nathan asked Jesus into his heart this year.

***Point your kids in the right direction—***
***when they're old they won't be lost.***

Proverbs 22:6, MSG

THIRTY-THREE

# The Power of Words

IT WAS QUIET in the house. Too quiet. Normally, four-year-old J.P. followed me from room to room. But I had gotten engrossed in a good book and suddenly realized I didn't hear his familiar noise. I panicked. How long had he been missing?

"Jason! Jason! Jason Paul Kent—where are you?"

No answer.

I quickly checked the kitchen, the bathroom, the living room and then dashed up the stairs to his room. At the time we were living in a unique old home with unusual architecture. The house had built-in cabinets, bookshelves, and closets everywhere—lots of places for a preschooler to hide. Running to J.P.'s room, I again called out, "Jason! Please answer me. Honey, *where are you?*"

I opened his closet door. In this rambling old house, J.P.'s closet had steps that led to the unfinished third-story attic. The dust was thick up there, but the previous owner loved train sets, and he had built a huge track that encircled the entire perimeter of the third floor. The attic, with its unfinished wood, old nails, and precarious drop-offs, was a dangerous place for a four-year-old.

Normally, the attic was closed off, but J.P. claimed ownership of this special room with the secret entrance in his bedroom and referred to it as "*my* attic." He often begged to explore this forbidden, poorly ventilated room.

Breathlessly, I ascended the stairs to the attic hideaway and opened the door. My child was nowhere in sight. He had simply disappeared.

I called his name out again and again with no answer. I ran to my bedroom across the hall so I could telephone Gene and try to figure out what to do. I knew the police wouldn't come. He'd been missing such a short time. I was feeling desperate! As I grabbed the phone, I heard a sound coming from the closet in the master bedroom. I bolted across the room and opened the door.

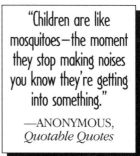

> "Children are like mosquitoes—the moment they stop making noises you know they're getting into something."
>
> —ANONYMOUS, *Quotable Quotes*

*There he was*—seated on the floor of the closet. He had found a pair of my pantyhose and somehow managed to pull them on—over the top of both tennis shoes and over the top of his blue jeans. The waist of the pantyhose was right around his little belt. In retrospect, it was a very humorous sight, but laughter was *not* the first thought on my mind. He had deliberately chosen not to respond to my calls and had caused me severe anxiety.

He instantly recognized the irritated look on my face and before I could open my mouth, he looked deeply into my eyes, smiled, and with an innocent, pleading, high-pitched voice he said, "My legs are soft, Mom—just like yours!"

I realized that at four years old J.P. was already learning the power of using the right words to dissipate a tense situation.

When my birthday rolled around last April, J.P. forgot my special day. When his card arrived a week late, it pictured a shy little boy on the front with a sheepish grin, holding a card in his outstretched hand. I opened it up and the words before me read: "Will you forgive me for being late if I remind you of how cute I am?" Then in small print at the bottom of the card, he wrote, "Honest, Mom, you do not seem to have aged at all in my mind. Happy Birthday!"

***Worry weighs us down;***
***a cheerful word picks us up.***

Proverbs 12:25, MSG

THIRTY-FOUR

# Jonathan's Story

THE UNEXPECTED phone call came from one of the producers at Focus on the Family. After reviewing one of my talks, they were requesting permission to broadcast it.

The night before the program was aired on sixteen hundred radio stations across the United States and Canada, I received the edited copy. I soon realized Jonathan Mutz's story would be heard all over the country the next day, and although the family had given me permission to tell others about their experience, I needed to let them know about the broadcast. Their answering machine answered my call, and I left a message.

It all began when I was invited to stay in the home of Pam and Bill Mutz. It was quickly obvious that these two were great parents, giving their three children abundant, unconditional love combined with the right amount of discipline. Sitting at their table, first for dinner and then for family devotions, was an education in itself. Everyone participated—including me.

The next day I asked my hostess what made their home so special. She told me that a few years earlier, she was bathing Cari, who was two and a half, and Jonathan, who was

seven months old. That week Pam and Bill had an out-of-town guest who had brought two dogs with him that were left outside in the yard. While Pam was bathing her children, she became concerned that the barking dogs might stray too far from the house and wake up the neighbors.

Jonathan had been sitting up well on his own, and Pam turned to Cari and said, "Honey, the dogs are barking outside. Wait just a minute while Mommy goes to get them."

> "A bird does not sing because he has an answer—he sings because he has a song."
>
> —JOAN ANGLAND, quoted by Tim Hansel in *You Gotta Keep Dancin'*

Pam was gone a short time, but when she returned, Jonathan was under water. Cari hadn't realized the danger. Pam grabbed her son and screamed for the guest, who came down and did mouth-to-mouth resuscitation while Pam called for an ambulance.

"They laid my Jonathan on a stretcher and worked feverishly over him, but even before we reached the hospital, I knew that he was gone," she said. In the days that followed, friends and family gathered, feeling Pam and Bill's grief as their very own.

I asked Pam about the long-term effect of this crisis point in their home. She said, "Carol, God has done an emotional and spiritual healing here that even psychologists do not understand. We know it's the Lord."

Several weeks after Jonathan had gone to be with the Lord, Pam and Cari were returning home in the car from running errands. Cari was playing with a helium balloon they had bought while shopping. Suddenly, she exclaimed, "Mommy, Mommy, open the window!"

Pam replied, "Cari, if I open the window, the balloon will—"

Cari insisted, "Mommy, Mommy, open the window!" So, Pam opened the window and as she did, Cari kissed the balloon, pushed it out the window and looking toward heaven said, "Here, Jesus, give this to Jonathan and tell him it's from Cari!" She joyfully let it go as tears rolled down Pam's cheeks.

This helium balloon tradition still continues in the Mutz family. As a result, a dear friend of the family once told Pam, "Someday when you see Jonathan in heaven, I think he'll greet you with an armful of balloons!"

Two months after returning home, I opened my mail and enjoyed a wonderful letter from Pam. Enclosed with the note was this entry from her quiet-time notebook:

Jonathan,

Tell me, my son, what are you doing on this beautiful, heavenly spring day?

Are you romping through the tall fields of grass, playing hide-and-seek with the other children in heaven?

Or are you sitting quietly by a babbling brook meditating on the miracles that God has accomplished in your young life?

Could you possibly be on kitchen assignment washing pans for the Master?

Or are you sitting at His feet praising God Almighty with your angelic voice?

Does our Lord tell you each time when we ask Him to communicate the precious "I love you's" and kisses we send?

Does He tell you how much we miss you and all the precious thoughts and words that Cari speaks of you?

Have you seen your new brother? Has God shown you his picture and told you all the stories of the cute things he has done? I know that they must make you chuckle!

Jacob would love to play trucks with his big brother for hours on end!

Does Jesus tell you that we cry tears for you?

You are our flesh and blood . . . our precious boy . . . at home with the best house-parent, Jesus. But we miss you so much! Mom cries tears of longing anticipation to once again hold her baby in the presence of our Jesus.

We love you, Jonathan. We love you very, very much.

Your Mom,
Pam

When I initially told the story, I realized that this remarkable couple chose to trust God, even if in this lifetime they were not allowed to know *why* this tragedy had happened.

At this writing Pam and Bill have nine living children and Jonathan in heaven. Shortly after their story aired on "Focus on the Family," Pam wrote the following note:

Dear Carol,

Your message brought much joy to our hearts. . . . Our family listened together on the water bed to the message you shared on "Focus on the Family." It was a very special time for us. . . .

Two weeks later we celebrated Jonathan's fourteenth birthday. As all of us surrounded his birthday cookie, we sang "Happy Birthday to Jonathan." The little ones blew out his candles and we lifted up a prayer of thanksgiving that Jonathan is with Jesus.

We went around the table and asked each child what they would most want to ask Jonathan in heaven and what they were thankful for concerning him. The replies were varied indeed:

- "Jonathan, what did it feel like when you were drowning?"
- "What's it like to be with Jesus *all day* and in

His presence *all the time?*"

☞ "Do you have a girlfriend up there?"

☞ "I'm thankful that Mom and Dad and Cari had Jonathan for seven months and that he didn't die at birth."

Now, that is the truth and it's definitely seeing the cup half full instead of half empty. . . .

At the end of Jonathan's birthday party, we signed and kissed a helium balloon and we all went outside to watch it rise on a starry, cold winter night. It went up *so slowly* because of the low temperature. We pictured even more in our minds how far up there Jonathan and Jesus are—and how Jesus will hand it to him on his special birthday. . . .

Love,
Pam

This remarkable family lives out the definition of "expectant hope."

***What a God we have! And how fortunate we are to have Him, this Father of our Master Jesus! Because Jesus was raised from the dead, we've been given a brand-new life and have everything to live for, including a future in heaven—and the future starts now! God is keeping careful watch over us and the future. The day is coming when you'll have it all—life healed and whole.***

***I know how great this makes you feel,***
***even though you have to put up with every kind***
***of aggravation in the meantime.***
***Pure gold put in the fire comes out of it***

proved *pure; genuine faith put through this suffering comes out* proved *genuine. . . .*

*You never saw him, yet you love him. You still don't see him, yet you trust him—with laughter and singing. Because you kept on believing, you'll get what you're looking forward to: total salvation.*

1 Peter 1:3-9, MSG

THIRTY-FIVE

# High Heels and Tennis Shoes

AFTER MONTHS OF PLANNING, we were on our way to the Grand Canyon. The first day on the road was all that our family had hoped for. During day two, the temperature topped one hundred degrees, and the weatherman said there was no sign of a change in the near future. For two full days J.P. had been saying, "Are we almost there yet?"

I was driving at the end of that second long day when we entered Amarillo, Texas. The sign on a local motel flashed "Luxury for Less." Oh, I wanted that! The line underneath it was equally impressive: Clean and Comfortable. I wanted *that*, too.

My husband went in, put our money on the counter, signed the registration form, and obtained our room key. When we stepped through the door, we consoled ourselves by pointing out that it *did* have beds and there *was* a shower—the two preestablished requirements for home away from home on this trip.

As we got the last suitcase out of the trunk and into the motel room, the top of the door fell off its hinge. Little Texas critters were making their way across the floor. The air conditioning had two levels, "very low" and "off"; but we were in cattle country, so an open window would have invited barnyard smells into the room. Turning back the covers on the beds, I discovered huge holes in the linens. (If you are from Texas, please don't be offended. I have visited your state on several occasions and realize you have many outstanding hotels. In this case, we had *chosen* low-budget accommodations.)

I wanted to leave, but my husband said, "We've paid our money, and we're staying!" It was one of those times when he had nonverbally said, "The end. Amen. Case closed. Don't bring it up again!" By the next morning, the members of our happy, dynamic Christian family were barely speaking to one another. We silently packed the suitcases into the car, and with the exception of answering the questions of young J.P., we spent the entire last day of the trip with no laughter, no fun, no conversation, and no music.

Later that day we stopped at one of the viewing points along the south rim of the Grand Canyon. We parked the car and prepared to get our first glimpse of the sight. I was wearing sandals with heels on them, and I had every intention of putting on my tennis shoes, which were in the back seat.

> "Never take a cross-country car trip with a kid who has just learned to whistle."
>
> —JEAN DEUEL, *A Rainbow of Hope*

At that moment my husband looked at me and broke the silence: "Surely you don't plan to see the Grand Canyon in high heels!"

Something in his tone made me decide that I *did* plan to see the Grand Canyon in high heels. We got out of the car and walked several feet toward the viewing point on very rocky terrain. I soon realized that I *could not* see the Grand Canyon in high heels.

I swallowed my pride and meekly asked my husband to retrieve my tennis shoes from the car. *Irritation* is not quite the word to describe what he was feeling at that point. *Exasperation* might come closer.

I'm sure Gene planned to throw the shoes *to* me rather than *at* me, but one of them hit me in the chest and the other one went flying beyond me. A young couple passing by us attempted to hide their amusement. In my humiliation I burst into tears, ran back to the car, and threw myself into the front seat as I shouted, "I've never wanted to see this dumb old canyon anyway. You and J.P. go look at it; I'll be waiting here in the car!"

My poor husband! We had traveled for three days in one-hundred-degree heat, and his wife was refusing to see the object of the entire trip. For several minutes he and J.P. stood outside the car waiting for me to quiet down and come to my senses.

Soon I heard our son say, "Daddy, *please* tell Mommy you're sorry!"

Since I wasn't climbing out, they decided to climb in. We had not begun the day with the Lord—it's very hard to have family devotions when the family members aren't speaking to one another. They said they were sorry; I said I was sorry; and together we told God how sorry we were for our terrible attitudes and lack of communication with Him and with one another. As we finished, we exchanged hugs and shed a few more tears, this time for the right reason. I put on my tennis shoes, and hand in hand we started walking toward the canyon.

When we arrived at the edge of that gorgeous panorama of color, space, depth, and beauty, we were momentarily speechless. The pictures in *National Geographic* had not done it justice. I have never seen anything so breathtaking in my life!

We soon found out there was an echo in the canyon. Immediately, the words to a much-loved song of praise and testimony, "How Great Thou Art," came to me. So we adapted the lyrics and formed a "yelling chorus." Holding hands and standing along the rim of the canyon, we shouted into that massive space, "O MIGHTY GOD, HOW GREAT THOU ART!" And we heard the creation echo back to the Creator the wonder and majesty of who He really is! It was one of the most spectacular moments of my lifetime, and I almost missed it because of a bad attitude.

*If you've gotten anything at all*
*out of following Christ,*
*if his love has made any difference in your life,*
*if being in a community of the Spirit*
*means anything to you, if you have a heart,*
*if you* care*—then do me a favor:*
*Agree with each other. . . .*
*Do everything readily and cheerfully—*
*no bickering, no second-guessing allowed!*
*Go out into the world uncorrupted,*
*a breath of fresh air in this squalid*
*and polluted society. Provide people*
*with a glimpse of good living*
*and of the living God.*

Philippians 2:1-2,14-15, MSG

THIRTY-SIX

# Daddy, Why Did Grandma Die?

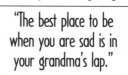

ONE OF THE HARDEST things we adults have to do in life is explain death to children, especially the death of someone they love.

A few years ago I was invited to speak at several Christian Women's Clubs in southwestern Ohio. At one of these I met Vada Duff, a vibrant woman who truly *loved* people. Laughter, compassion, and prayer were her calling cards. She was known for cinnamon rolls, an open door, a listening ear, a smile on her face, and an encouraging word.

> "The best place to be when you are sad is in your grandma's lap."
>
> —JEANNIE, AGE SEVEN, *When You Lick a Slug, Your Tongue Goes Numb*

Three years later Vada called, and when I asked how she was she told me, without self-pity, that it had been a good but challenging year. She had breast cancer. Because of Vada's optimism, I never knew how serious the cancer was—until she was gone.

Many people loved Vada, including a precious nine-month-old grandson named Andrew. Andrew's father is a physician, and he wrote an open letter in answer to his son's inevitable future question, "Daddy, why did Grandma die?"

Dear Andrew,

There are times in our lives that are difficult. Some things are hard to understand. At times, I think you are closer to God in your untainted, unspoiled innocence than many of us who have spent a lifetime seeking His face.

Andrew, as you know, we have prayed for Grandma Duff. And we have asked people to pray who have never had the pleasure of knowing Grandma. She was in the hospital and we knew that someday she'd be home. God answered our prayers—just not like we'd hoped. But still, He answered.

God invited Grandma to live with Him forever in heaven, and as much as she loves all of us, and as much as she found joy in you, she loves God more—and now there is more joy in heaven. Last Saturday she accepted God's invitation.

Andrew, don't be sad, because Grandma has lots of friends here with us who are very good at doing the things that grandmas are supposed to do.

In November 1990 your mommy and I told Grandma you were on the way. Despite the fact that cancer had made her right leg weak, she jumped high in the air. And at that moment, she began to love you.

In July, when you were born, Grandma made the three-hour trip to Toledo in two and a half hours. She was talking on the car phone to all of her friends the entire time—just to tell them *you* had finally arrived!

Andrew, somewhere around your one-month birthday, she decided on her nickname for you. She called you "Sugarplum." I don't know where she got that one, but it was her name for you. She even looked forward to the day you might be on the basketball team in high school so that she could stand up and yell, "Go, Sugarplum!"

Grandma had faith that she would see the things for

which she hoped. Grandma never talked about the cancer in her body. She always looked forward.

Last Friday night Grandma prayed as she fell asleep. "Dear Jesus, take this vision I have and watch me through the night." Andrew, I know the central focus of Grandma's vision was to share the love of her Lord Jesus with everyone. We remain here to remind everyone of that love.

Andrew, it seems not a day goes by that I do not have to tell one of my patients that I have found cancer in his or her body. It is a dreaded disease, *but it has its limits*.

I once read:

Cancer is so limited . . .
It cannot cripple love.
It cannot shatter hope.
It cannot corrode faith.
It cannot eat away peace.
It cannot destroy confidence.
It cannot kill friendship.

Cancer is so limited . . .
It cannot shut out memories.
It cannot silence courage.
It cannot invade the soul.
It cannot reduce eternal life.
It cannot quench the spirit.
It cannot lessen the power of the resurrection.[1]

Everything we face in this life has limits. The only thing I know that is *unlimited* is our heavenly Father's love for us and my love for you.

I Love You,
Dad*

*Dr. David Miller

*As parents feel for their children,*
*GOD feels for those who fear him.*
*He knows us inside and out,*
*keeps in mind that we're made of mud.*
*Men and women don't live very long;*
*like wildflowers they spring up and blossom,*
*But a storm snuffs them out just as quickly. . . .*
*GOD's love, though, is ever and always,*
*eternally present to all who fear him,*
*Making everything right for them and their children*
*as they follow his Covenant ways*
*and remember to do whatever he said.*

Psalm 103:13-18, MSG

*We headed for Sunday school. My sister Joy and her family were visiting us for the weekend, and we bundled the kids up and jumped into the car. My nephew K.C. was in kindergarten and, when we got to church, he decided he was brave enough to visit the class for his age group, even though he didn't know anybody in Aunt Carol's church. I was relieved to find out my good friend Marilyn would be his teacher. I knew K.C. would be in good hands.*

*An hour later the Sunday school classes were dismissed, and we picked up K.C. Later, as we stood in the lobby following the church service, Marilyn tapped on my shoulder and whispered, "Does your nephew live on a farm?" I was surprised by the question.*

*"Yes," I said. "My sister and her husband are renting a little farm and felt it would be good experience for the children to raise a couple of goats and some chickens. K.C. has daily chores with the animals. Why do you ask?"*

*Marilyn smiled. "I thought so," she said.*

*Marilyn had been teaching the story of Noah's ark. She painstakingly explained to the children how large the ark was and that two of every kind of animal got on this big boat before the Great Flood. Then she explained how long they were on the ark before they landed on top of Mount Ararat.*

*K.C.'s eyes got bigger and bigger. As Marilyn finished the story, she asked, "Does anybody have a question?"*

*K.C.'s hand shot up in the air. Fresh from his personal experience with animals and farm chores, he did have a question! "Teacher," he said intensely, "what I want to know is who had to clean up all that poop?"*

*A good question. An honest question.*

*Many of us are so familiar with the Bible that we forget to see the miracles in it. We get hung up on being "right" and appropriate and so we fail to honestly engage with the Teacher. We stare at the obstacle and never envision the opportunity.*

PART EIGHT

# When You Need Hope

THIRTY-SEVEN

# Project 23

THE PHONE RANG. I picked up the receiver and soon realized the voice on the other end of the line was the public school superintendent. Why would he be calling me *now?* I had taught drama, speech, and English at Fremont Junior High School for four years before giving birth to my beautiful son, Jason Paul. I had left the school system the year before to be a stay-at-home mother. Why would the head administrator be calling me?

He spoke distinctly. "Carol, there is an opening for a teacher at the Project 23 House, and I'm wondering if you would be interested in that position. I feel what's been lacking in that program to date is any kind of spiritual emphasis, and I feel you could bring that element to the girls who are enrolled in the program."

My heart leaped. Newaygo County had instituted an educational program for unwed pregnant teenagers a few years before. The plan was for young women throughout the county to be given the opportunity of entering a different kind of educational program during their pregnancies and for the semester following the birth of their babies. Their high school subjects were individualized so they could remain in school during the time many teen girls drop out.

The program was affectionately referred to as "Project 23" because two aging house numbers (a two and a three) dangled precariously by the side of the front door. The old house, which was adjacent to currently developed school property, had been purchased for future expansion. The house offered a home setting while the girls continued their education and learned how to care for their babies at the same time. They lived in their own homes and were bussed to the Project House five days a week. All of the students were either pregnant or new mothers. Those with newborns often brought their babies to school with them.

With my passion for evangelism and my love for young people, I immediately knew that if the details could be worked out, this combination of a job and a ministry was *perfectly* suited to my gifts. A Christian couple that lived only a few blocks from the Project House was available to care for J.P. during the hours I would be with the girls. Within a week, I knew God had opened every door for me to become the director of the Alternative Education Program for Pregnant Teenagers. I was ready to take on a new mission.

School would be starting just after Labor Day, and I readied the Project House for its occupants. The dining room, with its big table, was our main classroom. The kitchen provided the perfect spot for classes in nutrition. The living room was well suited for small group activities and counseling, and the remaining room became my office. Before school started I went through the house and prayed in each of the rooms, asking that God's presence would permeate every corner of the Project House.

On the first day of school, I arrived early and stood in the living room at Project 23. I prayed again: "Lord, thank You for this incredible job. As each of my students enters this home, help her to feel Your presence and to know that no matter what she's been through or how worthless she feels, that You love her and have a plan for her life and for that of her baby, far beyond what she sees right now. Help her to value the life of that baby and to know that no matter what her current circumstances are, You can give her a reason to go on.

"Lord, help me to love the least desirable girl who comes through this door in the same way I care for the most charming and personable young woman. Let my students see You in me and help them to be drawn to the Savior."

I didn't know it then, but over the next two years sixty-eight teenage girls would come and go through the doors at Project 23. During my last year of directing the program, seven of my students were only fourteen years old. They were barely out of puberty and already having babies.

> "There are people around us whom God longs to touch through us—people that only we can reach with our particular style and personality, people whom we have been called to. We must begin to ask God, 'Is this the one? Is she the one you are seeking?' It is a fantastic drama, and God wants to use us to accomplish it."
>
> —REBECCA PIPPERT, *Out of the Saltshaker*

At times my mission seemed wondrous. I was able to speak freely of the value of life and bring in people representing adoption agencies. Nutrition experts donated their services to train the girls. A myriad of doctors and nurses and health specialists gave of their time to affect young lives at Project 23.

At other times I felt hopeless. Slowly, I realized that listening was even more important than teaching at the Project House. The more comfortable the girls were with me and with each other, the more honest they became. Some of their comments still linger in my heart:

> "I have never heard my parents say the words 'I love you' to me. I planned this pregnancy so I could finally have somebody love me back."

> "This is my second baby. I killed my first one with an abortion. I felt so guilty I decided to have this one to make up for the one I murdered."

That fall I attended a Winning Women Retreat at Western Michigan University. Ann Kiemel was speaking. She was different from any speaker I'd heard before. Instead of presenting a typical talk with an introduction, outline, and conclusion, she sat on a bar stool near the edge of the stage and shared a series of illustrations regarding people she had met during her everyday life. She spoke of writing a note of encouragement, attaching it to a coffeecake, and placing it on the doorstep of someone who needed an uplift. She told of singing a few bars of a song to people who needed to be reminded that God still cares, in spite of current circumstances. Frequently, her stories didn't have endings that told what happened after her encounter with each individual.

God used the weekend to refresh my tired soul, to remind me that a simple act of kindness and showing genuine love are sometimes more powerful messages than when I dump the whole plan of salvation on someone's plate in one helping. I come from the "buttonhole them for Jesus" generation and had worked in youth ministries where the mission was considered unsuccessful if no one accepted Christ that day. Ann Kiemel's idea of "planting seeds of kindness and love," without necessarily attaching a little sermon, was a new concept.

The next Monday morning I arrived at the Project House to find that two of my students were there early. They were sitting around the kitchen table discussing how hard motherhood was.

One said, "I thought little babies just ate and slept, and all my baby does is cry!"

The other responded, "I know what you mean. The father of my baby has already taken off, and being a mother is hard work!"

I thought they sounded like middle-aged women instead of young teenagers. Thinking back to the weekend, I spoke up and said, "Girls, I've just learned the neatest little song. It sounds like you could use a lift today. Do you mind if I sing it to you?"

Jackie, the more sarcastic of the two, looked up and sneeringly said, "You want to sing a song—on *Monday morning*? You have got to be kidding!"

Jeannie rolled her eyes toward me and then back at Jackie as she patronizingly said, "Oh, come on, let's let her sing."

I looked at the two of them, eyeball to eyeball, and began to sing the song I'd heard Ann sing on the weekend. "God loves you and I love you, and that's the way it should be." I paused in my musical message to say, "Jackie and Jeannie, I *do* love you. You know that's true." I continued with direct eye contact and sang the last phrase of the song. "God loves you and I love you, and that's the way it [is]."[1]

I didn't know if I got the words or the tune right, but it didn't matter. The tears were streaming down Jeannie's cheeks and in her next breath she said, "I haven't been to church in a long time. Do you think you could pick me up so I could go to church with you next Sunday?"

Jackie wasn't weeping, but in her own hard way she had been moved by the song too. Her self-esteem was so low it was hard for her to make eye contact. Her family was an unusual mix of too many aunts, uncles, and cousins living under one roof. I wondered about what levels of sexual abuse and incest she might have encountered. She looked at me out of the corner of her eye as she said in a gruff tone,

"You know, I haven't been to church in a long time either. Do you think you could pick me up too?"

When I got home that day, I called everybody I could think of and asked them to pray for Jackie and Jeannie. I was exuberant. God could do a miracle in the lives of my students. And two of them were coming to church next Sunday. God was at work in the Project 23 House!

When Sunday morning arrived, I dressed hurriedly and jumped into the car. Both girls were ready on time, with their tiny babies in their arms. We talked and laughed as we made the trip to church. We dropped the babies off at the nursery and entered the church sanctuary.

I marched Jackie and Jeannie down to the front row. I wanted God to get His best shot at them. As the service progressed, I prayed . . . and waited . . . and waited . . . and waited. The pastor did an outstanding job. The gospel message was clear and the sermon was easy to follow. During the invitation, I waited again, expectantly, and nothing happened. *Nothing*.

I don't know if Jackie or Jeannie ever received Christ, but I know they heard His message of love and forgiveness and that they were given an opportunity. I've learned that God's timetable in people's lives is often different from mine . . . and I pray that the seed sown in Jackie's and Jeannie's hearts has been watered and nurtured and will one day bear fruit. No act of kindness or show of love is ever wasted. God is always at work, even when we can't see it.

***Who do you think Paul is, anyway?***
***Or Apollos, for that matter?***
***Servants, both of us—***
***servants who waited on you***
***as you gradually learned to entrust your lives***
***to our mutual Master.***

*We each carried out our servant assignment.*
*I planted the seed, Apollos watered the plants,*
*but* God *made you grow.*
*It's not the one who plants or the one who waters*
*who is at the center of this process but God,*
*who makes things grow.*
*Planting and watering are menial servant jobs*
*at minimum wages. What makes them worth*
*doing is the God we are serving.*
*You happen to be God's field*
*in which we are working.*

1 Corinthians 3:5-9, MSG

THIRTY-EIGHT

# Crossroads

I WAS MISERABLE.

It was the end of summer, 1977. Gene had accepted a new position with an insurance company in Fort Wayne, Indiana, and I was unhappy about it. Moving from my home state of Michigan was bad enough, but I was also leaving the most meaningful and fulfilling job I had ever had as director of the Alternative Education Program for Pregnant Teenagers in Newaygo County. It seemed so unfair.

By the time our move was complete, school had started. I talked to the administrator of Fort Wayne Christian School and found out there was still an opening for a teacher in the English department. After an interview, I was offered the position.

Once again, my heart became entangled in the lives of students, including Linda. She was bright, wise beyond her years, articulate, and an extraordinary writer. But something was wrong. Depressed, she would become silent and reclusive. Her ruminations seemed to be filled with self-analysis and soul-searching.

We talked often. Driven by perfectionism, Linda felt she could never live up to the expectations of herself and others. At times Linda felt like she was at the end of her rope.

At the end of that academic year, I left teaching to assume a ministry position in a local church. Within a year, we moved back to Michigan, but Linda has kept in touch ever since.

Last summer I received a fax from her. She wondered if she could meet me for lunch while I was speaking in the area.

It was a remarkable experience to be reunited with a former student after seventeen years. Linda had earned her bachelor's degree, with a double major in sociology and psychology. She had gone on to pursue a master's degree in social science. My onetime needy student had as many academic credentials as I did. In her current position she helps students and alumni in their career planning and placement. I felt a sense of deep fulfillment as I saw the maturity of this former student who was now my friend.

During our time together Linda said something that caught me by surprise. "That was a great interview they did on you in *Today's Christian Woman* magazine this year. I had the cover of that issue, with your picture on it, framed for my office because you were the person who saved my life when I was at a major crossroads in high school." It was time for me to leave for the airport to catch my return flight. Still reeling from this startling revelation, I quickly prayed with Linda and asked her to send me the story of what she went through during our year together in Fort Wayne.

Days later, this fax arrived on my desk:

> Dear Carol,
>
> It was December 1977, right before the Christmas holiday. Like many teenagers, I was angry and distraught. I was sitting in my room late one night after an argument. . . . I had taken as much as I thought I could

bear. I grabbed a knife. Sobbing and thinking that no one would find me until morning, I attempted to slit my wrist. I wanted to die.

What happened next was divine intervention. The extremely sharp knife, which had just been pressed and dragged across the veins in my left wrist, did not break through the skin. There was not even a scratch. I sat in wonder and amazement, baffled at the miracle I had just witnessed, wishing it hadn't happened to me. I wondered why God had spared me from the damage of the knife's blade.

Tears continued to flow and I was paralyzed for a moment. Confused, yet astonished, I wondered why God had chosen to intervene in my life. The question that hung over my consciousness was, "Why me?"

The next day I went to school and sought you out. You were a teacher I loved and respected. I shared my story with you, uncertain of what your reaction might be. Would you believe me? Would you tell my parents? Would you reject me for the actions I had taken? Or would you simply love me?

Deep down, before I ever sought you out, I knew what your response would be. You always smiled and told me that God loved me and you loved me. Sometimes you sang songs to me as we walked down the hallways of school together. I remember feeling embarrassed. But more importantly, I felt loved and that I was important to you and to God. Knowing that God loved me made all the difference in the world. No one had ever told me that I was important to God before. I mean, why would *He* need *me* when there are so many gifted and talented people in the world?

The words you shared on that snowy Indiana day, in a trailer classroom, have left an indelible impression on my heart which has forever changed my life. You told me that Satan would not be fighting for my life so persistently except for the fact that God was going to do something awesome through my life for His kingdom . . . SOMETHING AWESOME FOR GOD'S KINGDOM! That phrase rang over and over in my mind. For a teenage girl with low self-esteem, that was a new and foreign concept. But I believed you! Praise God, I believed you. *SOMETHING AWESOME FOR GOD'S KINGDOM* —that is truth, from the heart of God through the mouth of His servant to my ears.

Those words ring in my ears to this day, and my life has become an adventure of seeking out God's purpose. An adventure in service to the King and His kingdom. Suicide is no longer an option for me because I am on a journey. I have a major purpose. Satan cannot have the victory in my life, because I belong to God and He has something special for me to do.

Jeremiah 29:11-14 has become my life's verse. "'For I know the plans I have for you,' declares the LORD, 'plans to prosper you and not to harm you, plans to give you hope and a future. Then you will call upon me and come and pray to me, and I will listen to you. You will seek me and find me when you seek me with all your heart. I will be found by you,' declares the LORD."

In retrospect, I now know God orchestrated the people who were part of my life for a very special purpose. I live my life day by day with the truth that God can use one person with a heart willing to serve Him to make an impact on the life of another. Thank you for being that person in my life.

Day by day,
Linda

*GOD, my God, I yelled for help*
*and you put me together.*
*GOD, you pulled me out of the grave,*
*gave me another chance at life*
*when I was down and out.*

Psalm 30:2, MSG

*You're my cave to hide in,*
*my cliff to climb.*
*Be my safe leader,*
*be my true mountain guide.*
*Free me from hidden traps;*
*I want to hide in you.*
*I've put my life in your hands.*
*You won't drop me,*
*you'll never let me down.*

Psalm 31:3-6, MSG

THIRTY-NINE

# A Love Story

LONELINESS. LONGING. DESIRE. The heart of every human being yearns for love. To be fully understood by someone else. To be accepted with imperfections. To be valued and esteemed. To communicate without words.

As I talk to women across the United States and Canada, I've met many very content and happy single women who have had those needs met through significant friendships. But I've also met many unhappy single women. Not all single women wish they were married, but when there *is* a longing for marriage and no man on the horizon, the ache in the heart can be acute.

Gene and I had been married about a year when we moved to a little town in western Michigan. I was teaching in an area junior high school; Gene and I served as youth directors in our local church. We were excited about the opportunity of working with so many energized and needy young people. We began recruiting volunteers to help coordinate special events and chaperone our growing number of teenagers. One of our most enthusiastic volunteers was Sue.

Sue was in her twenties and worked in medical records at the local hospital. She was attractive, talented, and highly motivated. We became close friends after a short time. One day Sue seemed troubled and asked if I had time to talk.

We sat down and she hesitantly stated what was on her mind. She began, "Would you be willing to pray about something that's important to me?"

"Sure!" I responded quickly. "I would be happy to!"

She went on, "Ever since I was a little girl I looked forward to the day I would be married. I lined up my baby dolls in the nursery, gave them names, and pampered them. I was their mother. I always anticipated the day I would be a *real* mother. I actually *enjoy* working in the church nursery, and I *love* to cook. If any woman was ever well suited for marriage and for raising a family, it's me!"

I nodded, but said very little. She continued, "I haven't had a meaningful date in the last seven years, and sometimes I wonder if God cares about this longing in my heart. Carol, are you willing to pray with me—that God will bring a husband into my life?"

It was easy to see the direction this conversation was moving, but I was still a bit surprised by the question. If I prayed for Sue about a husband, she would begin *expecting* a man to come into her life soon, and I didn't want my friend to be disappointed in God and disillusioned with the power of prayer.

We were in a very small town. I didn't know of any Christian or nonChristian men in the area who were single and in the right age category to date Sue, much less match her education, intelligence, and spiritual maturity. Finding a man for Sue seemed a bit like asking God to create *something* out of *nothing!*

After a pause that was a bit too long, I replied, "Sue, I will definitely pray with you about this desire, but I want to ask you if you are willing to pray in a different way. I know God could provide exactly what you are looking for, but I also believe He may choose to meet your need in another way. Have you considered the value of being single? You have time to devote to God's work, and your life is rather unencumbered compared to women we both know who are changing diapers and trying to balance their home and work responsibilities at the same time." (I felt guilty for giving the pat response she'd heard from other Christians, but I didn't know what else to say!)

She nodded as I continued. "Are you willing to ask God to fill the void in your life either through providing a Christian husband or through leading you to a ministry or job that would be so fulfilling it would take away the emptiness in your heart?"

I could tell it was difficult for her to settle for anything less than a husband, but she voiced her agreement and we bowed our heads and prayed. As the next few weeks passed, we continued to pray. When we were together, we prayed aloud about this desire. When we were apart, we prayed individually.

> "When we pray we step inside the room of the general headquarters of God. We may enter through Jesus who is the Way. Our inability meets God's ability, and then miracles happen."
>
> —CORRIE TEN BOOM, *Clippings from My Notebook*

A few months later my husband and I entered the sanctuary on a Sunday morning. We sat in a pew near the back of the church. It was a small congregation, and I scanned the crowd to see who was there. As my eyes swiftly gazed toward the right side of the auditorium, I noticed a tall, handsome hunk sitting next to one of the widow ladies in our church. I wondered where he had come from. At that moment my eyes turned in the other direction, and I saw Sue in a pew a few rows in front of me. She, too, had noticed the attractive stranger and was staring in his direction.

Suddenly, she looked back at me, and we both looked in the direction of the mysterious visitor. In perfect unison we looked back at each other, smiled, and winked, as if to say, "Is this the man we prayed for?"

After some investigation, we learned that the young man was Lee, the son of the widow. He had pursued his education and had been established in business in another city. His father had passed away and his mother was in poor health. Lee knew his mother would have great difficulty relocating at this stage of life, and he decided to return home so he could provide care for her during her declining years. He soon became established in a local business and joined our church.

Six months later I was the matron of honor at Lee and Sue's wedding. Today, they are the proud parents of a son and a daughter, and they are actively involved in church leadership. One year they sent a Christmas card with a family picture on the front. As I observed the joy on their faces, I was reminded of the power of prayer.

***Are you hurting? Pray. Do you feel great? Sing. . . .***
***Make this your common practice:***
***Confess your sins to each other***
***and pray for each other. . . .***
***The prayer of a person living right with God***
***is something powerful to be reckoned with.***

James 5:13,16, MSG

FORTY

# Tiny Tim

THE FOLLOWING STORY was told to me by Sharon Dunsmore. It shows the consequences of sinful choices and the reality of God's grace.

It was a relatively calm day in the NICU (neonatal intensive care unit). I was on duty with two other nurses, and we were trying to have a conversation amidst the customary sounds of ventilators and heart monitors. Occasionally an alarm would go off, and one of us would attend to the needs of a tiny patient. In this arena of life and death we often exuded an ambivalent calm while executing our split-second decisions.

I was in mid-sentence when the shrill ring of the phone halted all conversation. It was the *red* phone, and *I* was leaning against it. The red phone was the emergency line between us and the labor and delivery room—very unobtrusive, unless it rings.

I fought the desire to walk away and let someone else answer it as I picked up the receiver. "Come fast," the voice said urgently. "We need a neonatal nurse *stat!*"

The other nurses looked at me and said, "You're on. We'll watch your patient here and set up for another admission."

Fear gripped my heart as I ran through the back entrance toward the delivery room. The labor and delivery nurses were ready when I arrived. Holding gown, gloves, and mask, they helped me into uniform and almost pushed me into the delivery room. When I didn't even get to "scrub in," I knew the situation was critical.

My adrenaline was up as I heard the sound of screaming and crying. Physicians and other staff members were giving orders. "Lord," I prayed, "give me wisdom and help the life or lives that are being threatened."

I made eye contact with the circulating nurse and asked, "What's happening here?"

She responded with little emotion. "It's an 'oops abortion,' and now it's your problem!" (In hospital talk an "oops abortion" means the mother's due date was calculated inaccurately; she was further along than expected, and the baby survived.)

The pediatrician ran by me with the fetus (now called a baby) in his hand. He swore and then yelled in my direction, indicating he wanted me to follow him into the resuscitation room adjoining the delivery room.

I looked into the bed of the warmer as I grabbed equipment. Before my eyes was a baby boy. A very, very tiny baby boy. The doctor and I immediately made an attempt at intubation (inserting a tube down the trachea from the mouth or nose of the infant to the tip of the lungs to ventilate, expand, and oxygenate the lungs). This procedure was unsuccessful and put the baby in much greater trauma. I glanced at the doctor and hesitantly asked, "Will you attempt intubation again?"

"You've got to be kidding," he replied. "It would be inhumane to attempt to intubate this poor little thing again.

This infant will never survive."

"No, Doctor, I'm not kidding," I said, "and it's my job to ask."

The doctor softened for a moment. "I'm sorry, Sharon. I'm just angry. The mother doesn't want the inconvenience of a baby, so she comes to the hospital so she can pay somebody to get rid of it—all neat and tidy. Then the whole thing gets screwed up when the fetus has the audacity to survive."

His words tumbled out. "Then everybody takes it seriously and calls the pediatrician, who's supposed to fix it or get rid of it. Then it's all on my shoulders, including the liability of this new unwanted little person!" With anger in his voice, he went on, "The lawyers will fight for the right to do whatever we want to our bodies, but watch out for what they will do when these abortions aren't so neat and tidy! A failed homicide—an 'oops'! Then all of a sudden everybody cares and it's turned from a 'right' into a 'liability' that someone gets the blame for."

As the doctor's emotions surged, he continued. "It's the last guy with his or her hands on this 'pro-choice entity' who now gets to be responsible for the 'oops.'" With sarcasm in his voice he said, "Well, Sharon, today that's you and me. We are the lucky shift, and I answered my phone and you answered your phone. Lucky us, huh?"

I spoke quietly. "This is pretty upsetting, isn't it?" As our eyes met, the doctor and I shared an unspoken anguish. We worked feverishly over the infant, doing everything that could be done according to the policy and standards of practice in our hospital—but we both knew we were losing the battle for the life of this baby.

We looked at our pathetic little patient. He was lying in the fetal position in the wrong environment, trying to get air into underdeveloped lungs that couldn't do the job. In a calmer voice, the doctor said, "Okay, nurse, I'm going back to the office. Keep him comfortable and let me know when it's over. I'm sorry about this. Call me if you need me. I know this is a hard one. If it helps, please know it's tough for me, too."

I watched the doctor retreat and then glanced back at the infant before me. He was struggling for oxygen. "Lord, help!" I prayed.

Almost instinctively, I took the baby's vitals. His temperature was dangerously low. I pushed the warmer settings as high as they could go. His heart rate was about 180–200 beats per minute. I could count the beats by watching his little chest pulsate. I notified the intensive care unit that we wouldn't be coming and that we would be waiting it out right where we were. All of the same life-saving equipment available to me in the Neonatal ICU was right here—and I knew the baby's time was short.

I settled down a bit and began to focus on this tiny little person who had no name. Suddenly, I found myself speaking to the baby: "Tiny Tim, who are you? I am very sorry you weren't wanted. It's not your fault. You didn't ask for this and neither did I."

I placed my little finger in his hand and *he grasped it*. As I watched him closely, I marveled that all the microscopic parts of a beautiful baby were present and functioning in spite of the onslaught.

I touched his toes and discovered he was ticklish! He had a long torso and long legs. I wondered if he would have become a basketball player. Perhaps he would have been a teacher or a doctor.

Emotions swept over me as I thought of my friends who had been waiting and praying for years for a baby to adopt. I spoke aloud once again to the miniature baby. "They would have given you a loving and a happy home. Why

would people destroy you before ever considering adoption? That goes beyond selfishness and turns into something sinister. Ignorance is *not* bliss, is it, Tiny Tim?"

He put his thumb into his mouth and sucked. I hoped it gave him comfort. My dialogue with the baby continued. "I'm sorry, Tim. I don't know how we got to be such a screwed-up society. There are people who would risk their lives for a whale or an owl before they even blink about what just happened to you."

> "Let my heart be broken by things that break the heart of God."
>
> —BOB PIERCE, quoted in *A Rainbow of Hope*

Tiny Tim was gasping and his little chest was heaving as if a truck was sitting on it. I took my stethoscope and listened to his tiny, pounding heart. I heard the swishing sound of a heart murmur. At the moment it seemed easier to focus on physiology rather than to be with this baby as a dying human being.

The baby wet. And with that action my mind took off again. Here was Tiny Tim with a whole set of kidneys, a bladder, and connecting tubes that functioned with a very complex system of chemistry. It was all working! He was an amazing little person! I turned the overhead light up and Tim turned from it, in spite of eyelids that were fused together to protect his two precious little eyes. I thought about his eyes. They would never see the sunset, the trees, a mother's smile, or the wagging tail of a dog.

I took his temperature again. It was dropping. He was gasping for air and continued to fight for life. I stroked him gently and began to sing, "Jesus loves the little children, all the children of the world. Red and yellow, black and white, they are precious in His sight. Jesus loves the little children of the world."[1] My spirit was still troubled.

A nurse walked in. "The doctor is on the phone and he wants to know what's happening."

I looked up and simply said, "Tiny Tim is dying, that's all. I will call when it's over, and it's not over."

The nurse responded, "It's so hot in here. How can you stand it?" I looked at the clock. One hour had gone by. She continued, "Can you stay over with this one? It's almost shift change."

"Sure. I'll stay," I replied. "He's been breathing like he's run a marathon and he keeps on struggling." I paused. "How's the mother doing?"

"Oh, she's fine. She's back in her room resting. The family said they don't want to see or hear about anything. They said, '*Just take care of it!*'" The nurse retreated with one last glance at the tiny patient. "For such a little person, he's sure putting up a big fight."

I looked at Tiny Tim and wondered if he knew that what he was fighting so hard for was *life*—and I knew he was losing it. He was dying and his family was *resting*. Their words tormented me. *Just take care of it!* No muss and no fuss.

The clock was moving very slowly. I had turned off the audio signals on the alarms because they would have been going off constantly. I wondered if I should have left them on as a signal to the world that all is *not* well! I wanted to stand on a soapbox and yell at the top of my lungs, "Something serious is happening! Does anybody care? A baby is dying here, and this shouldn't be happening!"

Tiny Tim moved and caught hold of my baby finger again, and I just let him hang on. I didn't want him to die without being touched and cared for. As I saw him struggling for air, I said, "It's okay, Tim. You can let go. You can go back to God."

His gasping started slowing down, along with his other vitals, but he still clung to my finger. Nurses stopped in to check on his progress, and another call came from the doctor. He found it upsetting that this whole thing was taking

so long. I knew the doctor was living with the same agony I was experiencing. I tried to remember why I chose this profession and couldn't.

I stroked the baby ever so slowly, and he gently curled around my finger in the fetal position. I watched him take his last breath and then spoke softly, "Goodbye, Tiny Tim. You *did* matter to someone."

(Shortly after this incident, Sharon left the neonatal intensive care unit and accepted a new position as the manager of a psychiatric unit.)

One day a young female came to be admitted into the unit. She was severely depressed and had made one unsuccessful suicide attempt. As I interviewed her, the patient kept her head down, and she was almost nonverbal. Her appearance was haggard and her demeanor sad, yet she was beyond crying. Her clothes didn't match and smelled, indicating a total neglect of hygiene. She rocked back and forth slowly. Despite her wasted appearance, I saw a hint of beauty and intelligence.

I could tell the admission process was going to take a long time. After a while, Kathy began to speak. She had gone through an abortion three years before and had been looking for "something" for a long time, but didn't know what it was. She was having recurring nightmares. A baby was crying for help and kept calling her name. In her dreams Kathy searched for the baby, but could never find it.

She began to fill her days with workaholism and perfectionism. She was obsessed by a need for extreme cleanliness and excessive organization. Her efforts exhausted her.

Every time she saw a baby, she searched the tiny face for some kind of recognition. If she was near a crying infant, she would soon be shaking and in tears. In an attempt to cover her pain, she shopped and spent money she didn't have. Creditors and bill collectors followed her everywhere.

Kathy confessed, "I began using sleeping pills to chase away the insomnia and the dreams. The pills didn't work, but I'd wake up the following day in a stupor that kept me in a confused and irritable state of mind. I lost my friends. Then I lost my job. Then I began to drink alcohol with a different group. They said, 'Come on, just a few drinks. Let's party and you'll feel better.' I didn't. Nothing could get rid of the pain and the searching. And things got worse."

By this time Kathy was like a volcano, erupting with fiery emotion. She couldn't speak fast enough. She continued, "One day, when I thought I couldn't go any further physically or mentally, I decided to kill myself. I didn't know how to do it, but I took a bunch of pills and just went to sleep."

Her deep, dark eyes softened. Looking up, she said, "Do you know what it feels like to decide to die and have no one in your life who really cares? No one should have to die alone. I tried to, but I couldn't even do *that* right!"

She began to cry and I thought she would never stop. Kathy fell into my arms and curled up like a baby. She continued sobbing uncontrollably until she was consumed with exhaustion. I held her for a long time and rubbed her back, as I had done with my own children.

As she calmed down, I said, "Kathy, I care about you, and you *are* important. God doesn't make mistakes, and I think you're a beautiful person. Tell me what happened. When were you hurt? Where's the baby?"

She stared up at me with a look of wonder. Perhaps she felt accepted by another human being for the first time. I don't know. But her eyes changed to a look of total openness and honesty. I could tell she was no longer afraid of me. Pausing momentarily, I said, "Are you ready to talk about it tonight, or do you need more time?"

"No, please," she responded, "I've got to tell somebody. I've never said it before. I'm tired of running from it." And Kathy began her story.

She had gotten pregnant at a very inconvenient time. Her fiancé was in the middle of a career change. Her parents had always used guilt to control her. Since the doors of parental communication were closed, she went to an abortion clinic on the advice of her boyfriend and coworkers. All the voices of influence around her said, "Just take care of it. It's no big deal."

At the clinic the doctor said the gestation was early and there would be no problem. She was scheduled for a d. and c. on an outpatient basis. But soon after getting into surgery, things were not as *easy* as had been promised. The gestational age of the fetus had been inaccurately figured, and Kathy went into labor. Chaos ensued and she was transferred to the delivery room.

Kathy remembers hearing a baby cry. Doctors and nurses were racing around. She screamed, "What's wrong?"

One of the nurses responded, "You're having a baby!"

Kathy recoiled and screamed, "No!"

A nurse came into her room much later to tell her and her family that the baby died. The nurse quietly asked if she would like to hold her baby and say goodbye. Kathy said the word *baby* shocked her. In all of her talks with the people at the clinic, the fetus was never referred to as a *baby*. She didn't want to hear the word and mentally put it out of her mind.

Family members responded to the nurse. "No, just take care of it and don't come back."

Kathy said, "I remember the eyes of the nurse as she looked at me and said, 'Is that what *you* want?' In my heart I wanted to see the baby, but my family assured me it was best to say no. I was confused and I just wanted to have it all over with."

Her voice was filled with emotion. "I never got to see my baby." Kathy put her head in her hands and cried softly again. Through tears, she continued, "I don't even know if it was a boy or a girl. No one told me."

After several weeks of intensive therapy and high doses of antidepressants, Kathy was making progress. She was a pretty woman and had an interesting personality. As time went on, she cried less often, but it was a very painful experience for Kathy to deal with so much unresolved conflict. After keeping her story bottled up for three years, she began verbalizing more of the details connected with her unexpected pregnancy and the ensuing failed abortion.

I agonized with her. This was a fragile time for Kathy. As time passed, she began putting in specific names and places. She used the name of the hospital and the names of doctors.

As I continued working with Kathy, a disturbing realization dawned on me. It couldn't be! But it was.

I compared her dates and events with my own three-year-old calendar and came to an amazing realization: *Kathy was Tiny Tim's mother*.

Because of hospital regulations, I couldn't tell her what I knew at that time, but I wanted to shout: "You had a beautiful baby. He was a little boy, and he *did* have a name—Tiny Tim! He had blond hair and long legs. He didn't die alone. He was loved and cared for and prayed over."

In my heart, as one mother to another, I knew I could give some semblance of peace to this young woman who so desperately needed the missing pieces of a major puzzle in her life. When the time was right, I knew I would tell her about Tiny Tim.

Time passed. I was no longer a nurse or a therapist. She was no longer a psychiatric patient. We met in a restaurant. Two human beings with a small segment of history in common. The meeting was awkward. Uncomfortable. Emotional. Painful. No last names, addresses, or phone numbers were exchanged.

I gently unfolded the story that had been hidden for so long. Tears flowed as I gave Kathy the gift of answers. Her baby was touched and loved by a mother. He was given a name. He didn't die alone. He was sent back to a loving God.

> "The voice of sin may be loud, but the voice of forgiveness is louder."
>
> —D. L. MOODY, *Great Quotes and Illustrations*

As the visit neared an end, we held each other and wept. I looked into Kathy's eyes and saw a new strength and calm. There were scars, but she was beginning to heal. The nightmares were put to rest. We hugged and parted, knowing we would probably never meet again in this lifetime.

Sometimes I wonder why God allowed me to care for these two special human beings. Tiny Tim's pain didn't last long, but it was fatal. Kathy's pain almost cost her her life and is a wound that will take years to fully heal. The scar will last forever. A *choice* that was intended to be "no big deal" turned out to be *a very big deal* for all of us.[2]

*GOD made my life complete*
*when I placed all the pieces before him.*
*When I got my act together,*
*he gave me a fresh start.*
*Now I'm alert to GOD's ways;*
*I don't take God for granted.*
*Every day I review the ways he works. . . .*
*I feel put back together,*
*and I'm watching my step.*
*GOD rewrote the text of my life*
*when I opened the book of my heart*
*to his eyes.*

Psalm 18:20-24, MSG

# Afterword: What About Your Stories?

Recently, a friend told me about a remarkable answer to prayer. I listened with rapt attention as she described the way circumstances and people came together at precisely the right moment. Her eyes sparkled with the wonder of what had occurred and she simply said, "*It was a 'God-thing*.'" I understood.

Most of us have experiences that bring laughter and sometimes tears on a daily basis. At times God uses our children to teach us profound truth. Most often our *crisis points* provide a platform upon which He helps us develop an eternal perspective. This book was not written to "milk your emotions." It was penned to help you develop the daily habit of looking for God in unexpected places. If you laughed out loud during some of the stories and wiped a tear during others—I know you identified with the life lessons in the illustrations.

How can *you* put this principle to work in your life and in your family? Take a moment each day (or once a week) to write down a *growing experience* or a *humorous situation* you've had recently. You may not yet understand what God had to do with the event, but write it down anyway.

Then respond to the following questions:

1. What emotions did I experience while living through this situation?
2. What Scripture verse or passage comes to mind as I think about what took place?
3. What was the "life lesson" God taught me in this event?
4. How could my willingness to tell this story help another person?

If you have children, make a habit of discussing the "*God-thing*" they discovered during their day at school or at play. In what situation did they find God at work in their day? When families begin to communicate at this level, exciting things happen!

I also want to encourage you to share your stories with the rest of the world. If you have a humorous or inspirational story, poem, or incident from real life that you feel belongs in a future book like this, please send it to me.

Carol Kent
c/o Speak Up, Inc.
P.O. Box 610941
Port Huron, MI 48061-0941
FAX: (810)987-4163
PHONE: (810)982-0898

*Retreats, conferences, seminars:* You can also contact me at the above address for speaking engagements, for audio tapes, or for information on how to attend the communications training seminar, "Speak Up With Confidence."

Remember, detours make life more inspirational, worthwhile, and memorable. Keep taking them!

# Notes

**Why I Wrote This Book and What You'll Get Out of It**

1. Old Arab proverb, quoted by Mark R. Littleton, "Raisins in the Oatmeal: The Art of Illustrating Sermons," *Leadership* 4, no. 2 (Spring 1983), p. 66.
2. Quoted from Carol Kent, *Speak Up With Confidence* (Nashville: Nelson, 1987), p. 47.

**Chapter Eight: Husband for Sale**

1. Source unknown.

**Chapter Thirteen: The Policeman and the Purse**

1. "The Family of God," words by William J. and Gloria Gaither, music by William J. Gaither. Copyright 1970, William J. Gaither/ASCAP. All rights reserved. Used by permission.

**Chapter Twenty-Five: Do We Have to Move—Again?**

1. From: *Lord, It Keeps Happening . . . and Happening*, by: Ruth Harms Calkin © 1984. Used by permission. All rights reserved.

**Chapter Twenty-Six: Daisy's Best Advice**

1. Corrie ten Boom, as quoted by Cliff Barrows in the introduction of Corrie ten Boom, *Clippings from My Notebook* (Minneapolis: World Wide Publications, 1982), p. 2.

**Chapter Thirty-Six: Daddy, Why Did Grandma Die?**

1. Source unknown.

**Chapter Thirty-Seven: Project 23**

1. "God Loves You and I Love You," copyright 1976, Don Wyrtzen/Singspiration Music/ASCAP. All rights reserved. Used by permission of Benson Music Group, Inc., Nashville, Tenn.

**Chapter Forty: Tiny Tim**

1. "Jesus Loves the Little Children," words by Elsie Leslie.
2. Sharon Dunsmore, copyrighted unpublished story as told to author, 1995. Used by permission.

# Author

Carol Kent is the founder and president of "Speak Up With Confidence" seminars, a ministry committed to helping Christians develop their communication skills.

A member of the National Speakers Association, Carol is scheduled more than a year in advance to speak at conferences and retreats throughout the United States and Canada. She is also a frequent guest on a a wide variety of radio and television broadcasts, including "Focus on the Family," "Prime Time America," "Chapel of the Air," and "100 Huntley Street."

Carol has a B.S. degree in speech education and an M.A. in communication arts from Western Michigan University. Her background includes four years as a drama, speech, and English teacher, and two years as director of the Alternative Education Program for pregnant teenagers. After a brief time of working as a director of women's ministries at a midwestern church, she went into full-time speaking.

Carol's other books include *Secret Longings of the Heart, Tame Your Fears* (both NavPress), and *Speak Up With Confidence* (Thomas Nelson).

Carol and her husband, Gene, live in Port Huron, Michigan. They have one son, Jason, who is currently a student at the United States Naval Academy. They also have a temperamental Himalayan cat named Bahgi.